The
BRITISH RAIL
SPOTTER'S
COMPANION

The last surviving Class 45, No.45106 was brought south on 5th November 1988 by Pathfinder Tours. It is seen here leaving Southampton with the "Wessex Adventurer" en route to the Fawley branch.
(Brian Morrison)

The BRITISH RAIL SPOTTER'S COMPANION

1989

12th Edition

Compiled by

The NATIONAL RAILWAY
ENTHUSIASTS ASSOCIATION

Haynes

Oxford Publishing Co.

A FOULIS-OPC Railway Book

British Library Cataloguing in Publication Data
British Rail spotter's companion.—12th ed.
1. Great Britain. Railway services:
British Rail. Locomotives & multiple units – Lists
I. National Railway Enthusiasts Association

ISBN 0-86093-456-X

Library of Congress catalog card number
88-82690

Published by:
Haynes Publishing Group
Sparkford, Near Yeovil, Somerset. BA22 7JJ

Haynes Publications Inc.
861 Lawrence Drive, Newbury Park, California 91320, USA.

Printed by J. H. Haynes & Co. Ltd.

Front cover: **Class 73**: No. 73205 *London Chamber of Commerce* in revised InterCity livery, with the 11.15 Victoria–Gatwick at Stoat's Nest Junction, Coulsdon on 16 August 1988.
(Brian Denton)

Back cover: **Class 144**: Set Nos 144017 and 144009 (coach Nos 55817+55840 and 55809+55832) in the attractive West Yorkshire PTE livery at Skipton station on 28th May 1988.
(Les Nixon)

BRITISH RAIL DIESEL LOCOMOTIVES

CLASS 03 BRITISH RAIL SHUNTER 0-6-0

Built: 1958-62
Maximum Speed: 28 mph
Weight: 31 tonnes
Engine: Gardner 204 hp
Transmission: Mechanical
Route Availability: 1
Wheel Diameter: 3′ 7″
Maximum Tractive Effort: 15,300 lb

03073	BD	03162	BD	03170	BD

CLASS 08 BRITISH RAIL SHUNTER 0-6-0

Built: 1953-62
Maximum Speed: 15/20 mph
Weight: 50 tonnes
Engine: English Electric 400 hp
Transmission: Two English Electric Traction Motors
Route Availability: 5
Maximum Tractive Effort: 35,000 lb
Wheel Diameter: 4′ 6″

08011	BY	08414	SF	08454	WN	08499	YK
08202	CF	08415	AN	08460	NC	08500	YK
08308	TI	08416	TO	08463	DY	08506	TE
08309	HO	08417	SF	08466	BS	08507	GD
08375	CF	08418	DR	08472	CD	08508	TI
08388	IM	08419	CL	08479	CF	08509	TI
08389	NL	08421	GD	08480	OC	08510	DR
08390	LE	08428	DY	08481	CF	08511	DY
08393	SF	08434	TI	08482	AN	08512	GD
08397	IM	08436	TI	08483	BR	08514	DR
08399	DY	08440	SF	08484	ZN	08515	GD
08401	IM	08441	GD	08485	AN	08516	HO
08402	AN	08442	GD	08489	GD	08517	BS
08405	IM	08445	IM	08492	TI	08519	TE
08407	NC	08447	CL	08493	CF	08521	GD
08410	BR	08448	DY	08495	CA	08523	OC
08411	TE	08449	IM	08496	CA	08525	YK
08413	SF	08451	WN	08498	NC	08526	CA

08527	SF	08591	AY	08646	LE	08696	WN
08528	CA	08593	SF	08647	DL	08697	TO
08529	CA	08594	CA	08648	WN	08698	SF
08530	NC	08595	YK	08649	OC	08699	CD
08531	SF	08597	TO	08650	EH	08700	BS
08532	AN	08599	CD	08651	OC	08701	GD
08533	SF	08601	● BS	08652	CF	08702	CD
08534	CL	08603	BS	08653	OC	08703	AN
08535	BS	08604	BS	08654	CF	08704	BY
08536	DY	08605	YK	08655	SF	08705	CA
08537	IM	08607	DR	08656	BY	08706	HO
08538	CA	08609	WN	08657	YK	08707	HO
08539	CA	08610	BS	08658	NC	08708	NC
08540	CA	08611	LO	08659	HO	08709	SF
08541	SF	08612	WN	08660	CF	08710	HA
08542	SF	08613	CD	08661	NL	08711	CA
08543	TI	08614	WN	08662	YK	08712	PH
08544	GD	08615	AN	08663	LA	08713	CA
08556	OC	08616	BS	08664	CF	08714	CA
08561	AY	08617	WN	08665	IM	08715	SF
08562	● DR	08618	GD	08666	LO	08717	IS
08565	ML	08619	LO	08667	NL	08718	HA
08567	YK	08620	ML	08668	CF	08719	YK
08568	ML	08622	ML	08669	AN	08720	HA
08569	AN	08623	TO	08670	WN	08721	LO
08570	HA	08624	LO	08672	BS	08723	DR
08571	HA	08625	WN	08673	LO	08724	SF
08573	WN	08627	SF	08675	AY	08725	ML
08575	TE	08628	BY	08676	LO	08727	AY
08576	LA	08629	ZN	08677	WN	08729	DR
08577	GD	08630	ML	08680	AB	08730	HA
08578	GD	08631	● CA	08682	DR	08731	ML
08580	CA	08632	IM	08683	WN	08732	ML
08581	ML	08633	CD	08685	NC	08733	ML
08582	TE	08634	OC	08686	AN	08734	IM
08583	YK	08635	CD	08688	AN	08735	AY
08584	LA	08637	CF	08689	SF	08737	CD
08585	CD	08638	CA	08690	CL	08738	ML
08586	AY	08641	LA	08691	TI	08739	CD
08587	GD	08642	ZG	08692	● BS	08740	SF
08588	TE	08643	BR	08693	AY	08741	GD
08589	CF	08644	LA	08694	CD	08742	CD
08590	NL	08645	LA	08695	CD	08743	IM

08744	SP	08790	LO	08835	CF	08884	AN
08745	NL	08791	HA	08836	CF	08885	DR
08746	CD	08792	LA	08837	OC	08886	GD
08747	GD	08793	HA	08838	DY	08887	WN
08748	SF	08794	NL	08839	LA	08888	GD
08749	TI	08795	GL	08840	LA	08889	CA
08750	SF	08796	CF	08841	BS	08890	WN
08751	IM	08797	GD	08842	DY	08891	LO
08752	NC	08798	LE	08843	CD	08892	ZG
08753	IS	08799	GL	08844	CL	08893	BS
08754	IS	08800	BR	08845	EH	08894	SP
08755	HA	08801	LA	08846	AN	08895	LE
08756	LE	08802	GD	08847	EH	08896	LE
08757	CA	08803	RG	08848	CF	08897	LE
08758	SF	08804	OC	08849	LA	08899	DY
08759	BS	08805	BS	08850	RG	08900	BR
08760	EH	08806	HO	08851	ML	08901	BS
08761	HA	08807	BY	08853	ML	08902	AN
08762	PH	08808	CL	08854	SU	08903	DR
08763	HA	08809	AN	08855	AB	08904	WN
08765	BS	08810	NC	08856	AN	08905	WN
08766	NL	08811	WN	08857	TI	08906	TE
08767	NC	08813	DR	08858	AN	08907	CD
08768	CL	08814	DY	08859	NC	08908	NL
08769	LE	08815	SP	08865	CA	08909	BY
08770	TE	08817	TE	08866	DR	08910	CL
08771	GD	08818	CF	08867	● TE	08911	CL
08772	● NC	08819	BR	08868	NC	08912	CL
08773	HO	08820	LO	08869	● NC	08913	CD
08775	NC	08821	OC	08870	TI	08914	BY
08776	HO	08822	CF	08871	IM	08915	LO
08777	YK	08823	CD	08872	GD	08916	AN
08778	GL	08824	DR	08873	SF	08917	AN
08780	LE	08825	WN	08874	NL	08918	AN
08781	GL	08826	CL	08875	NL	08919	TI
08782	HO	08827	CL	08876	DR	08920	BS
08783	HO	08828	SF	08877	IM	08921	CD
08784	CD	08829	TO	08878	TI	08922	BY
08785	CF	08830	EH	08879	TI	08923	SF
08786	TE	08831	EH	08880	TI	08924	AN
08787	CF	08832	BS	08881	HA	08925	SP
08788	DY	08833	SF	08882	AB	08926	WN
08789	BY	08834	SF	08883	ZH	08927	BY

08928	BS	08936	NC	08945	LA	08953	LA
08929	OC	08937	LA	08946	RG	08954	LA
08930	SF	08938	ML	08947	OC	08955	LA
08931	GD	08939	AN	08948	OC	08956	NC
08932	CF	08940	CF	08949	BR	08957	SF
08933	EH	08941	LA	08950	BR	08958	SF
08934	WN	08942	CF	08951	BR		
08935	BR	08944	OC	08952	ML		

●

08562	DR	The Doncaster Postman	08692	BS	Railfreight
			08772	NC	Camulodunum
08601	BS	Spectre	08867	TE	Ralph Easby
08631	CA	Eagle	08869	NC	The Canary

CLASS 08/9 FITTED WITH REDUCED CAB HEIGHT AND HEADLIGHT FOR BURRYPORT AND GWENDRAETH VALLEY LINE

08993	LE	Ashburnham (08592)	08995	LE	Kidwelly (08687)
08994	LE	Gwendraeth (08462)			

CLASS 09 BRITISH RAIL SHUNTER 0-6-0

***Built**:* 1959-61 ***Maximum Speed**:* 27 mph
***Weight**:* 50 tonnes ***Engine**:* English Electric 350 hp
***Transmission**:* Two English Electric Traction Motors
***Route Availability**:* 5
***Maximum Tractive Effort**:* 25,000 lb ***Wheel Diameter**:* 4′ 6″

09001	EH	09008	CF	09015	EH	09023	AF
09002	AF	09009	SU	09016	SU	09024	AF
09003	SU	09010	SU	09018	AF	09025	EH
09004	SU	09011	AF	09019	AF	09026	EH
09005	SU	09012 ●	SU	09020	SU		
09006	SU	09013	CF	09021	AF		
09007	SL	09014	SU	09022	AF		

●

09012	SU	Dick Hardy

CLASS 20 ENGLISH ELECTRIC TYPE 1 Bo-Bo

Built: 1957-68 ***Maximum Speed:*** 60 mph
Engine: English Electric 1000 hp ***Weight:*** 73-74 tonnes
Transmission: Four English Electric Traction Motors
Route Availability: 5
Maximum Tractive Effort: 42,000 lb ***Wheel Diameter:*** 3' 7"

20004		TO	20055		TO	20100		TO	20141		TO
20005		TO	20056		TO	20102		IM	20142		TO
20006		TO	20057		TO	20103		TO	20143		TO
20007		TO	20058		TO	20104		TO	20144		TE
20008		TE	20059		TO	20105		TO	20145		IM
20009		IM	20061		IM	20106		TO	20147		TO
20010		TO	20063		TO	20107		IM	20148		ED
20013		TO	20064		IM	20108		TO	20151		TO
20016		TO	20065		TO	20110		IM	20154		TO
20019		TO	20066		ED	20112		IM	20156		TE
20020		TO	20069		IM	20113		TO	20157		TO
20021		TO	20070		TO	20114		ED	20158		TO
20023		TO	20071		TO	20117		TO	20159		TO
20025		IM	20072		TO	20118	●	TE	20160		TO
20026		TO	20073		TO	20119		TE	20163		TO
20028		TE	20075		TO	20120		TO	20165	●	TE
20029		TO	20078		TO	20121		TO	20166		TO
20030		IM	20080		TO	20122	●	TE	20168		TO
20031		IM	20081		TO	20124		TO	20169		TO
20032		TO	20082		TO	20126		IM	20170		TO
20034		TO	20083		TO	20127		ED	20171		IM
20035		IM	20084		TO	20128		TO	20172		TE
20040		TO	20085		TO	20129		TO	20173		TO
20042		TO	20087		TO	20130		TO	20175		TO
20043		IM	20088		TO	20131		TO	20176		TO
20044		IM	20090		TO	20132		TO	20177		TO
20045		TO	20092		IM	20133		TO	20178		TO
20046		IM	20093		IM	20134		TO	20179		TO
20047		TO	20094		TO	20135		TO	20182		TO
20048		TO	20095		IM	20136		TO	20183		TO
20051		TO	20096		IM	20137	●	TE	20185		IM
20052		TO	20097		TO	20138		ED	20186		TO
20053		TO	20098		IM	20139		TO	20187		TO
20054		TO	20099		TO	20140		TO	20188		TO

20189	TO	20197	TO	20208	TO	20217	TO
20190	TO	20198	ED	20210	TO	20218	TO
20192	ED	20199	ED	20211	ED	20227	ED
20193	ED	20202	ED	20212	ED	20228	IM
20194	TO	20204	ED	20213	ED		
20195	TO	20205	ED	20214	TO		
20196	TO	20206	ED	20215	TO		

●

20118	TE	Saltburn by the Sea
20122	TE	Cleveland Potash
20137	TE	Murray B. Hofmeyr
20165	TE	Henry Pease

CLASS 26 BIRMINGHAM RAILWAY CARRIAGE & WAGON Co LTD TYPE 2 Bo-Bo

Built: 1958-59 ***Maximum Speed:*** 80 mph
Engine: Sulzer 1160 hp ***Weight:*** 75-79 tonnes
Transmission: Four Crompton-Parkinson Traction Motors
Route Availability: 5 or 6
Maximum Tractive Effort: 42,000 lb ***Wheel Diameter:*** 3′ 7″

26/0		26/1			
26001	ED	26021	ED	26037	ED
26002	ED	26023	ED	26038	ED
26003	ED	26024	ED	26039	ED
26004	ED	26025	ED	26040	ED
26005	ED	26026	ED	26041	ED
26006	ED	26027	ED	26042	ED
26007	ED	26028	ED	26043	ED
26008	ED	26031	ED	26046	ED
26010	ED	26032	ED		
26011	ED	26034	ED		
26014	ED	26035	ED		
26015	ED	26036	ED		

CLASS 31	BRUSH TYPE 2	AIA-AIA

Built: 1957-62 ***Maximum Speed:*** 80-90 mph
Engine: English Electric 1470 hp ***Weight:*** 107-113 tonnes
Transmission: Four Brush Traction Motors
Wheel Diameter: 3′ 7″ (Driven) 3′ 3½″ (Centre)
Maximum Tractive Effort: 42,800 lb ***Route Availability:*** 5 or 6

31/1		31152	SF	31205	IM	31259	BS
		31154	IM	31206	IM	31260	TE
31101	IM	31155	TI	31207	IM	31263	SF
31102	TI	31156	IM	31208	IM	31264	TE
31105	SF	31158	TI	31209	SF	31268	SF
31106	CD	31159	TI	31210	IM	31270	CD
31107	BS	31160	TI	31212	IM	31271	SF
31108	TI	31162	BS	31215	TE	31272	SF
31110	TI	31163	TI	31217	CD	31273	IM
31112	BS	31164	TI	31219	SF	31275	CD
31113	TI	31165	SF	31221	IM	31276	CD
31116	SF	31166	TI	31223	IM	31278	TE
31118	TE	31168	SF	31224	SF	31281	TE
31119	BS	31170	IM	31225	IM	31282	TE
31120	CD	31171	TI	31226	SFu	31283	TE
31123	TE	31173	SF	31229	TE	31284	TE
31124	SF	31174	TI	31230	CD	31285	TE
31125	TI	31178	BS	31231	SF	31286	TE
31126	TI	31180	TI	31232	IM	31288	BS
31127	SF	31181	SF	31233	IM	31289	BS
31128	SF	31184	TE	31234	SF	31290	CD
31130	CD	31185	IM	31235	BS	31292	CD
31131	TE	31186	SF	31237	BS	31293	BS
31132	TI	31187	SF	31238	IM	31294	SF
31134	SF	31188	IM	31240	SF	31296 ●	BS
31135	CD	31189	SF	31242	IM	31299	IM
31138	BS	31190	SF	31243	IM	31301	BS
31141	CD	31191	SF	31247	IM	31302	IM
31142	TI	31196	IM	31248	TI	31304	IM
31144	TI	31198	SF	31249	IM	31305	BS
31145	TI	31199	IM	31250	SF	31306	SF
31146	TI	31200	CD	31252	CD	31308	SF
31147	TI	31201	IM	31255	CD	31309 ●	TI
31149	SF	31203	IM	31257	CD	31311	SF

31312		CD	31319		IM	31322		IM	31324		CD
31317		BS	31320		SF	31323		SF	31327	●	SF

31/4 fitted Eth.

31400		CD	31418		CD	31435		BS	31454		BS
31402		TI	31419		BS	31437		BS	31455		BS
31403		BS	31420		BS	31438		CD	31456		IM
31404		BS	31421		CD	31439		IM	31457		IM
31405		BS	31422		BS	31441		IM	31458		IM
31406		BS	31423		BS	31442		CD	31459		BS
31407		BS	31424		BS	31443		CD	31460		IM
31408		CD	31425		CD	31444	●	IM	31461		IM
31409		BS	31426		CD	31445		BS	31462		BS
31410		CD	31427		CD	31446		BS	31463		BS
31411		BS	31428	●	CD	31447		IM	31464		BS
31412		CD	31429		CD	31448		BS	31465		BS
31413	●	BS	31430	●	BS	31449		IM	31466		TI
31414		CD	31431		IM	31450		CD	31467		TI
31415		BS	31432		IM	31451		BS	31468		BS
31416		CD	31433		BS	31452		IM	31469		IM
31417		BS	31434		BS	31453		IM			

●

31296	BS	Amlwch Freighter/Tren Nwyddau Amlwch
31309	TI	Cricklewood
31327	SF	Phillips-Imperial
31413	BS	Severn Valley Railway
31428	CD	The North Yorkshire Moors Railway
31430	BS	Sister Dora
31444	IM	Keighley and Worth Valley Railway

CLASS 33 BIRMINGHAM RAILWAY CARRIAGE & WAGON Co LTD TYPE 3 Bo-Bo

Built: 1960-2 ***Maximum Speed:*** 85 mph
Engine: Sulzer 1550 hp ***Weight:*** 78-79 tonnes
Transmission: Four Crompton-Parkinson Traction Motors
Route Availability: 6
Maximum Tractive Effort: 45,000 lb ***Wheel Diameter:*** 3′ 7″

33/0

33002		EH	33020		EH	33033		SL	33052	●	SL
33004		SL	33021		SL	33035		SL	33053		SL
33006		EH	33022		SL	33039		SL	33055		SL
33008	●	EH	33023		EH	33040		SL	33056	●	SL
33009		EH	33025	●	SL	33042		SL	33057		SL
33011		SL	33026		EH	33046		SL	33058		SL
33012		EH	33027	●	SL	33047		SL	33060		SL
33013		EH	33029		SL	33048		SL	33063		SL
33015		EH	33030		EH	33050		SL	33064		SL
33016		SL	33031		SL	33051	●	SL	33065		EH
33019		SL									

●

33008	EH	Eastleigh
33025	SL	Sultan
33027	SL	Earl Mountbatten of Burma
33051	SL	Shakespeare Cliff
33052	SL	Ashford
33056	SL	The Burma Star

33/1 Equipped for multiple working with EMU,TC stock and Class 73.

33101	EH	33107	EH	33111	EH	33116	EH
33102	EH	33108	EH	33113	EH	33117	EH
33103	EH	33109	EH	33114	EH	33118	EH
33106	EH	33110	EH	33115	EH	33119	EH

33/2 Built to Hastings line loading guage.

33201	SL	33204	SL	33207	SL
33202	SL	33205	SL	33208	SL
33203	SL	33206	SL	33211	SL

CLASS 37 ENGLISH ELECTRIC TYPE 3 Co-Co

Built: 1960-65
Engine: English Electric 55,500 hp
Route Availability: 5
Maximum Tractive Effort:
Transmission: Six English Electric Traction Motors

Maximum Speed: 80 mph
Weight: 102-120 tonnes
Wheel Diameter: 3′ 7″

37/0		37054	IM	37101	TI	37175	IS
		37055	SF	37104	SF	37178	SF
37003	TI	37057	SF	37106	IM	37184	ED
37004	SF	37058	TI	37107	SF	37185	TI
37009	TI	37059 ●	TI	37109	IS	37188 ●	ED
37010	ML	37062	TI	37110	IS	37190 ●	
37012	SF	37063	TI	37113	ED	(37314)	ML
37013	TI	37065	TI	37114 ●	IS	37191	ED
37015	TI	37066	TI	37116	SF	37194	TI
37019	SF	37069 ●	TE	37128	SF	37196	IS
37023	ED	37070	IS	37131	CF	37197	CF
37025	ED	37071	TI	37133	CF	37198	TI
37029	TI	37072	TI	37135	SF	37201	ML
37031	TI	37073	TI	37138	SF	37202	IM
37035	ED	37074	SF	37139	CF	37203	IM
37037 ●		37075	SF	37140	SF	37207	CF
(37321)	ML	37077	SF	37141	CF	37209	SF
37038	SF	37078	CF	37142	CF	37211	CF
37040	ML	37080	ED	37144	SF	37212	CF
37042	IM	37083	IM	37146	CF	37213	CF
37046	TE	37087	SF	37153	IS	37214	CF
37047	SF	37092	ML	37154	SF	37215	CF
37048	IM	37095	TI	37158	CF	37216	SF
37049 ●		37096	TI	37162	CF	37217	CF
(37322)	ML	37097	ED	37167	CF	37218	CF
37051	ML	37098	TI	37170	ED	37219	SF
37053	SF	37100	SF	37174	CF	37220	CF

37221		CF	37239		CF	37254		CF	37280		CF
37222		CF	37240		ED	37255		IM	37285		TI
37223		CF	37241		IM	37258		IM	37293		CF
37225		IM	37242		TI	37260	●	IS	37294		CF
37227		CF	37244		CF	37261	●	IS	37298		TI
37229		ED	37245		ED	37262	●	IS	37303		TI
37230		CF	37248		CF	37263		CF	37304		TI
37232		ED	37250		ED	37264		CF	37306		CF
37235	●	CF	37251		TI	37275		IM	37308		CF
37238		SF	37252		SF	37278		CF			

●

37037	ML	Gartcosh
37049	ML	Imperial
37059	TI	Port of Tilbury
37069	TE	Thornaby T.M.D.
37114	IS	Dunrobin Castle
37188	ED	Jimmy Shand
37190	ML	Dalzell
37235	EF	The Coal Merchants' Association of Scotland
37260	IS	Radio Highland
37261	IS	Caithness
37262	IS	Dounreay

37/3 Renumbered for use on British Steel trains in Scotland.

37310	ML	British Steel Ravenscraig
37311	ML	British Steel Hunterston
37312	ML	Clyde Iron
37313	ML	
37320	ML	Shap Fell
37323	ML	Clydesdale
37324	ML	Clydebridge
37325	ML	Lanarkshire Steel
37326	ML	Glengarnock

37350 (37119) CF
37351 (37002) IM
37352 (37008) TI
37353 (37032) TI
37354 (37043) SF
37355 (37045) TI
37356 (37068) TI Grainflow

37357 (37079) TI
37358 (37091) SF P&O Containers
37359 (37118) ED

37370 (37127) ML
37371 (37147) CF
37372 (37159) CF

37373 (37160) ML	37376 (37199) CF	37379 (37226) ML
37374 (37165) CF	37377 (37200) IM	37380 (37259) TI
37375 (37193) CF	37378 (37204) TI	37381 (37284) IM

37/4 fitted Eth.modified at Crewe.

37401	ED	Mary Queen of Scots
37402	ED	Oor Wullie
37403	ED	Glendarroch
37404	ED	Ben Cruachan
37405	ED	Strathclyde Region
37406	ED	The Saltire Society
37407	ED	Loch Long
37408	ED	Loch Rannoch
37409	ED	Loch Awe
37410	ED	Aluminium 100
37411	ED	The Institution of Railway Signal Engineers
37412	ED	Loch Lomond
37413	ED	Loch Eil Outward Bound
37414	IS	
37415	IS	
37416	IS	
37417	IS	Highland Region
37418	IS	An Comunn Gaidhealach
37419	IS	
37420	IS	The Scottish Hosteller
37421	IS	
37422	ED	
37423	ED	Sir Murray Morrison 1874-1948 Pioneer of the British Aluminium Industry
37424	ED	Isle of Mull
37425	ED	Sir Robert McAlpine/Concrete Bob
37426	ED	Y Lein Fach/Vale of Rheidol
37427	ED	Bont Y Bermo
37428	ED	David Lloyd George
37429	ED	Eisteddfod Genedlaethol
37430	ED	Cwmbran
37431	ED	Sir Powys/County of Powys

37/5 Refurbished with alternator replacing the main generator.

37501 (37005)	TE	Teesside Steelmaster
37502 (37082)	TE	British Steel Teesside
37503 (37017)	TE	British Steel Shelton
37504 (37039)	TE	British Steel Corby
37505 (37028)	TE	British Steel Workington
37506 (37007)	TE	British Steel Skinningrove
37507 (37036)	TE	Hartlepool Pipe Mill
37508 (37090)	TE	
37509 (37093)	TE	
37510 (37112)	TE	
37511 (37103)	TE	Stockton Haulage
37512 (37022)	TE	Thornaby Demon
37513 (37056)	TE	
37514 (37115)	TE	
37515 (37064)	TE	
37516 (37086)	TE	
37517 (37018)	TE	
37518 (37076)	TE	
37519 (37027)	TE	
37520 (37041)	TE	
37521 (37117)	TE	
37667 (37151)	TE	Wensleydale
37668 (37257)	TE	Leyburn
37669 (37129)	LA	
37670 (37182)	LA	
37671 (37247)	LA	Tre Pol and Pen
37672 (37189)	LA	Freight Transport Association
37673 (37132)	LA	
37674 (37169)	LA	William Cookworthy
37675 (37164)	LA	
37676 (37126)	TI	
37677 (37121)	TI	
37678 (37256)	TI	
37679 (37123)	TI	
37680 (37224)	TI	
37681 (37130)	TI	
37682 (37236)	TI	
37683 (37187)	TI	
37684 (37134)	TI	
37685 (37234)	TI	
37686 (37172)	TI	

37687 (37181)	TI		
37688 (37205)	TI	Great Rocks	
37689 (37195)	CF		
37690 (37171)	CF		
37691 (37179)	CF		
37692 (37122)	CF		
37693 (37210)	CF		
37694 (37192)	CF		
37695 (37157)	CF		
37696 (37228)	CF		
37697 (37243)	CF		
37698 (37246)	CF	Coedbach	
37699 (37253)	CF		

37/7 Refurbished with alternator replacing the main generator.

37701	(37030)	CF
37702	(37020)	CF
37703	(37067)	CF
37704	(37034)	CF
37705	(37060)	SF
37706	(37016)	SF
37707	(37001)	SF
37708	(37089)	SF
37709	(37014)	SF
37710	(37044)	CF
37711 ●	(37085)	CF
37712 ●	(37102)	CF
37713	(37052)	CF
37714	(37024)	CF
37715	(37021)	CF
37716	(37094)	CF
37717	(37050)	CF
37718	(37084)	CF
37719	(37033)	CF
37796	(37105)	CF
37797	(37081)	CF
37798	(37006)	CF
37799 ●	(37061)	CF
37800 ●	(37143)	CF
37801 ●	(37173)	CF
37802	(37163)	CF
37803	(37208)	CF
37883	(37176)	CF
37884	(37183)	CF
37885	(37177)	CF
37886	(37180)	CF
37887	(37120)	CF
37888 ●	(37135)	SF
37889	(37233)	CF
37890	(37168)	SF
37891	(37166)	SF
37892 ●	(37149)	SF
37893	(37237)	SF
37894	(37124)	CF
37895	(37283)	CF
37896	(37231)	CF
37897	(37155)	CF
37898	(37186)	CF
37899	(37161)	CF

●

37711	CF	Tremorfa Steelworks
37712	CF	The Cardiff Rod Mill
37794	CF	Sir Dyfed/County of Dyfed
37800	CF	Glo Cymru
37801	CF	Aberthaw/Aberddawan
37888	SF	Petrolea
37892	SF	Ripple Lane

37/9 Refurbished with manufacturers prototype power units.

37901	CF	Mirrlees Pioneer	37904	CF	
37902	CF		37905	CF	Vulcan Enterprise
37903	CF		37906	CF	

CLASS 45 BRITISH RAIL TYPE 4 1Co-Co1

Built: 1960-63
Maximum Speed: 90 mph
Engine: Sulzer 2500 hp
Weight: 135-138 tonnes
Route Availability: 7
Wheel Diameter: 3′ 9″, 3′ 0″
Maximum Tractive Effort: 55,000 lb
Transmission: Six Crompton-Parkinson Traction Motors

45/1

45106 TI

CLASS 47 BRITISH RAIL & BRUSH TYPE 4 Co-Co

Built: 1963-67
Maximum Speed: 95 mph
Engine: Sulzer 2580 hp
Weight: 117-125 tonnes
Wheel Diameter: 3′ 9″
Maximum Tractive Effort: 60,000 lb
Transmission: Six British Traction Motors
Route Availability: 6

47/0 built with boiler

47002		TI	47019		CD	47096		SF	47116		SF
47003		ED	47033		CF	47097		TI	47117		TI
47004		ED	47049		TI	47098		TI	47118		ED
47005		TI	47050		CD	47099		SF	47119	•	CD
47006		ED	47051		CD	47100		SF	47120		TI
47007	•	SF	47052		TI	47101		CD	47121		SF
47008		CD	47053		ED	47102		TI	47123		SF
47009		CD	47054		IM	47105		SF	47124		TI
47010	•	CD	47060	•	TI	47107		TI	47125	•	CD
47012		TI	47063		CF	47108		SF	47142	•	TI
47014		SF	47079		CF	47110		TI	47143		TI
47016	•	TI	47085	•	CD	47112		SF	47144		TI
47017		ED	47094		CF	47114		SF	47145		TI
47018		ED	47095		TI	47115		IM	47146		TI

47147		TI	47205		TI	47227		CD	47281		CF
47150		TI	47206		TI	47228		CD	47283	●	TI
47152		TI	47207	●	TI	47229		CD	47284		TI
47156		TI	47209		TI	47231	●	TI	47285		TI
47157		TI	47210		ED	47233	●	CD	47286		TI
47186		CF	47211		TI	47234		TI	47287		TI
47187		CD	47212		IM	47236		TI	47288		TI
47188		TI	47213		TI	47237		TI	47289		TI
47189		CD	47214	●	TI	47238	●	TI	47290		TI
47190	●	CD	47215		TI	47241		TI	47291	●	SF
47193	●	CD	47217		TI	47245		TI	47292		TI
47194	●	CD	47218		TI	47249		TI	47293		TI
47195	●	CD	47219		TI	47256		TI	47294		IM
47196	●	CD	47220		TI	47258		TI	47295		IM
47197		CF	47221		IM	47270		TI	47296		TI
47198		CF	47222	●	IM	47276		IM	47297		TI
47200		TI	47223		IM	47277		CF	47298		TI
47201		TI	47224		IM	47278	●	CD	47299		IM
47203		TI	47225		TI	47279		TI			
47204		TI	47226		TI	47280	●	TI			

●

47007	SF	Stratford
47010	CD	Xancidae
47016	TI	The Toleman Group
47060	TI	Halewood Silver Jubilee 1988
47085	CD	Conidae
47119	CD	Arcidae
47125	CD	Tonnidae
47142	TI	The Sapper
47190	CD	Pectinidae
47193	CD	Lucinidae
47194	CD	Bullidae
47195	CD	Muricidae
47196	CD	Haliotidae
47207	TI	Bulmers of Hereford
47214	TI	Tinsley Traction Depot
47222	IM	Appleby-Frodingham
47231	TI	The Silcock Express
47233	CD	Strombidae
47238	TI	Bescot Yard
47278	CD	Vasidae
47280	TI	Pedigree
47283	TI	Johnnie Walker
47291	SF	The Port of Felixstowe

47/3 built without train heat

47301		TE	47321		TI	47341		OC	47362		TE
47302		TE	47322		CD	47343		CD	47363	•	TE
47303		TE	47323		CD	47344		IM	47364		CD
47304		TE	47324	•	CD	47345		CD	47365	•	CD
47305		TE	47325		SF	47346		SF	47366	•	SF
47306		TI	47326		CF	47347		TE	47367		SF
47307		TI	47327		CF	47348	•	IM	47368	•	CD
47308		TI	47328		SF	47349		CD	47369		CF
47309		TI	47329		IM	47350	•	CD	47370		TI
47310		TI	47330		CD	47351		CD	47371		TI
47311	•	TI	47331		IM	47352		IM	47372		TI
47312		TI	47332		IM	47353		CD	47373		IM
47313		TI	47333		OC	47354		CD	47374		IM
47314		TI	47334		OC	47355		CD	47375		TI
47315		TI	47335		CD	47356		CD	47376		TI
47316		TI	47336		IM	47357		CD	47377		TI
47317	•	TI	47337	•	TI	47358		CD	47378		TI
47318		CF	47338		TI	47359		CF	47379	•	IM
47319	•	IM	47339		CD	47360		TI	47380	•	IM
47320		CF	47340		CD	47361	•	TE	47381		CF

•		
47311	TI	Warrington Yard
47317	TI	Willesden Yard
47319	IM	Norsk Hydro
47324	CD	Glossidae
47337	TI	Herbert Austin
47348	IM	St. Christopher's Railway Home
47350	CD	British Petroleum
47361	TE	Wilton Endeavour
47363	TE	Billingham Enterprise
47365	CD	ICI Diamond Jubilee
47366	SF	The Institution of Civil Engineers
47368	CD	Neritidae
47379	IM	Total Energy
47380	IM	Immingham

47/4 electric train heat

47401	IM	47406	IM	47411	IM	47417	IM
47402	IM	47407	IM	47413	IM	47418	IM

47421		TI
47422		CD
47423		CD
47424	●	CD
47425	●	CD
47426		CD
47427		CD
47428		CD
47430		SF
47431		CD
47432		CD
47433		SF
47434	●	CD
47435		SF
47436		CD
47438		CD
47439		CD
47440		CD
47441		CD
47442		CD
47443	●	CD
47444	●	CD
47445		CD
47446		CD
47447		CD
47448	●	CD
47449		CD
47450		CD
47451		CD
47452	●	SF
47453		CD
47454		CD
47455		SF
47456		CD
47457	●	CD
47458		SF
47459		CD
47460		IS
47461	●	IS
47462		SF
47463		CD
47465		SF
47466		BR
47467		IS
47468		BR
47469	●	IS
47470	●	ED
47471	●	CD
47473		LA
47474		TI
47475		CD
47476		BR
47477		BR
47478		CD
47479		CD
47481		CD
47482		SF
47483		CD
47484	●	OC
47485		CD

●

47424	CD	The Brontes of Haworth
47425	CD	Holbeck
47434	CD	Pride in Huddersfield
47443	CD	North Eastern
47444	CD	University of Nottingham
47448	CD	Gateshead
47452	SF	Aycliffe
47457	CD	Ben Line
47461	IS	Charles Rennie Mackintosh
47469	IS	Glasgow Chamber of Commerce
47470	ED	University of Edinburgh
47471	CD	Norman Tunna G.C.
47484	OC	Isambard Kingdom Brunel

47488	CD	Rail Riders
47489	BR	
47490	BR	Bristol Bath Road
47491	CD	Horwich Enterprise
47492	IS	The Enterprising Scot
47500	BR	Great Western
47501	BR	Craftsman
47503	CD	The Geordie
47508	BR	S.S.Great Britain
47509	CD	Albion
47512	CD	

47513	OC	Severn
47515	BR	Night Mail
47517	CD	Andrew Carnegie
47518	ED	
47519	BR	
47520	CD	
47521	CD	
47522	SF	Doncaster Enterprise
47523	SF	
47524	ED	
47525	BR	
47526	BR	
47527	CD	
47528	BR	
47530	CD	
47531	CD	
47532	CD	
47533	BR	
47534	BR	
47535	BR	University of Leicester
47536	BR	
47537	BR	Sir Gwynedd/County of Gwynedd
47538	BR	
47539	BR	Rochdale Pioneers
47540	BR	
47541	IS	The Queen Mother
47542	ED	
47543	BR	
47544	CD	
47546	IS	Aviemore Centre
47547	LA	
47549	ED	Royal Mail
47550	IS	University of Dundee
47551	BR	
47552	BR	
47553	CD	
47555	CD	The Commonwealth Spirit
47556	BR	
47557	BR	
47558	BR	Mayflower
47559	BR	Sir Joshua Reynolds
47560	BR	Tamar
47562	ED	Sir William Burrell

47563	IS	Womans' Guild
47564	BR	Colossus
47565	BR	
47566	BR	
47567	BR	Red Star
47568	BR	
47569	ED	
47570	ED	
47571	CD	
47572	BR	Ely Cathedral
47573	OC	The London Standard
47574	BR	Benjamin Gimbert G.C.
47575	BR	City of Hereford
47576	SF	King's Lynn
47577	CD	
47578	ED	The Royal Society of Edinburgh
47579	SF	James Nightall G.C.
47580	BR	County of Essex
47581	SF	Great Eastern
47582	OC	County of Norfolk
47583	OC	County of Hertfordshire
47584	BR	County of Suffolk
47585	BR	County of Cambridgeshire
47586	CD	
47587	LA	
47588	TI	Carlisle Currock
47589	CD	
47590	BR	Thomas Telford
47591	BR	
47592	BR	County of Avon
47593	ED	Galloway Princess
47594	TE	
47595	ED	Confederation of British Industry
47596	TI	Aldeburgh Festival
47597	ED	
47598	SF	
47599	TI	
47600	TI	Dewi Sant/Saint David
47602	CD	Glorious Devon
47603	CD	County of Somerset
47604	ED	Women's Royal Voluntary Service
47605	CD	
47606	CD	Odin

47607	CD	Royal Worcester
47608	CD	
47609	BR	Fire Fly
47610	CD	
47611	BR	Thames
47612	CD	Titan
47613	BR	North Star
47614	ED	
47615	TI	Castell Caerffili/Caerphilly Castle
47616	BR	Y Ddraig Goch/The Red Dragon
47617	ED	University of Stirling
47618	CD	Fair Rosamund
47619	CD	
47620	BR	Windsor Castle
47621	BR	Royal County of Berkshire
47622	ED	The Institution of Mechanical Engineers
47623	OC	Vulcan
47624	BR	Cyclops
47625	BR	
47626	BR	Atlas
47627	BR	City of Oxford
47628	OC	Sir Daniel Gooch
47629	BR	
47630	IS	
47631	BR	
47632	ED	
47633	ED	
47634	BR	Henry Ford
47635	IS	Jimmy Milne
47636	ED	Sir John De Graeme
47637	CD	Springburn
47638	CD	County of Kent
47639	CD	
47640	IS	University of Strathclyde
47641	IS	Fife Region
47642	IS	Strathisla
47643	IS	
47644	IS	The Permanent Way Institution
47645	CD	Robert F. Fairlie Locomotive Engineer 1831-1885
47646	CD	
47647	CD	Thor
47648	CD	

47649	ED	47654 ●	BR	47658	BR	47662	BR
47650	BR	47655	BR	47659	BR	47663	BR
47651	BR	47656	BR	47660	BR	47664	BR
47652	BR	47657	BR	47661	BR	47665	BR
47653 ●	BR						

●

47653	BR	Samson
47654	BR	Finsbury Park

47/7 push-pull fitted.

47701	ED	Saint Andrew
47702	ED	Saint Cuthbert
47703	ED	Saint Mungo
47704	ED	Dunedin
47705	ED	Lothian
47706	ED	
47707	ED	Holyrood
47708	ED	Waverley
47709	ED	The Lord Provost
47710	ED	Sir Walter Scott
47711	ED	Greyfriars Bobby
47712	ED	Lady Diana Spencer
47714	ED	Grampian Region
47715	ED	Haymarket
47716	ED	Duke of Edinburgh's Award
47717	ED	(47497)Tayside Region

CLASS 47/9 BRUSH TYPE 5 Co-Co

Modified at Crewe 1975/6 to 47/6 and again 1979/80 with Ruston Paxman engine.

47901 BR

CLASS 50 ENGLISH ELECTRIC TYPE 4 Co-Co

Built: 1967-68
Maximum Speed: 100 mph
Engine: English Electric 2700 hp
Weight: 117 tonnes
Route Availability: 6
Wheel Diameter: 3′ 7″
Maximum Tractive Effort: 48,500 lb
Transmission: Six English Electric Traction Motors

50001	LA	Dreadnought
50002	LA	Superb
50003	LA	Temeraire
50004	LA	St.Vincent
50005	LA	Collingwood
50007	LA	Sir Edward Elgar
50008	LA	Thunderer
50009	LA	Conqueror
50012	LA	Benbow
50015	LA	Valiant
50016	LA	Barham
50017	LA	Royal Oak
50018	LA	Resolution
50019	LA	Ramillies
50020	LA	Revenge
50021	LA	Rodney
50023	OC	Howe
50024	OC	Vanguard
50025	OC	Invincible
50026	OC	Indomitable
50027	LA	Lion
50028	LA	Tiger
50029	LA	Renown
50030	OC	Repulse
50031	OC	Hood
50032	OC	Courageous
50033	OC	Glorious
50034	OC	Furious
50035	OC	Ark Royal
50036	OC	Victorious
50037	OC	Illustrious
50039	OC	Implacable
50040	OC	Centurion
50041	LA	Bulwark
50042	LA	Triumph
50043	LA	Eagle
50044	LA	Exeter
50045	LA	Achilles
50046	OC	Ajax
50048	LA	Dauntless
50050	OC	Fearless

50/1 modified 1987.

50149	LA	Defiance

CLASS 56 BRITISH RAIL & BRUSH TYPE 5 Co-Co

Built: 1976-84
Engine: Ruston-Paxman 3250 hp
Route Availability: 7
Maximum Tractive Effort: 61,800 lb
Transmission: Six Brush Traction Motors
Maximum Speed: 80 mph
Weight: 125 tonnes
Wheel Diameter: 3' 9"

56001-30 built by Electroputere at Craiova, Roumania sub contracting for Brush

56001	●	CF	56033		CF	56065		TO	56097		TO
56002		TO	56034	●	CF	56066		TO	56098		TO
56003		TO	56035	●	CF	56067		TO	56099		TO
56004		TO	56036		CF	56068		TO	56100		TO
56005		TO	56037	●	CF	56069		TO	56101		TO
56006		TO	56038	●	CF	56070		TO	56102		TO
56007		TO	56039		CF	56071		TO	56103		TO
56008		TO	56040	●	CF	56072		CF	56104		TO
56009		TO	56041		CF	56073		TO	56105		TO
56010		TO	56042		TO	56074	●	TO	56106		TO
56011		TO	56043		CF	56075	●	TO	56107		TO
56012		TO	56044		CF	56076		TO	56108		TO
56013		TO	56045		CF	56077		TO	56109		TO
56014		TO	56046		CF	56078		TO	56110		TO
56015		TO	56047		TO	56079		TO	56111		TO
56016		TO	56048		CF	56080		TO	56112		TO
56017		TO	56049		CF	56081		TO	56113		TO
56018		TO	56050		CF	56082		TO	56114		TO
56019		TO	56051		CF	56083		TO	56115		TO
56020		TO	56052		CF	56084		TO	56116		TO
56021		TO	56053	●	CF	56085		TO	56117		TO
56022		TO	56054		TO	56086		TO	56118		TO
56023		TO	56055		CF	56087		TO	56119		TO
56024		TO	56056		CF	56088		TO	56120		TO
56025		TO	56057		CF	56089		TO	56121		TO
56026		TO	56058		TO	56090		TO	56122	●	TO
56027		TO	56059		TO	56091		TO	56123	●	TO
56028	●	TO	56060		TO	56092		TO	56124	●	TO
56029		TO	56061		TO	56093		TO	56125		TO
56030		TO	56062		TO	56094		TO	56126		TO
56031	●	CF	56063	●	TO	56095	●	TO	56127		TO
56032	●	CF	56064		TO	56096		TO	56128		TO

56129		TO	56131	●	TO	56133	●	TO	56135	● TO
56130		TO	56132	●	TO	56134	●	TO		

●

56001	CF	Whatley
56028	TO	West Burton Power Station
56031	CF	Merehead
56032	CF	Sir De Morgannwg/County of South Glamorgan
56034	CF	Castell Ogwr/Ogmore Castle
56035	CF	Taff Merthyr
56037	CF	Richard Trevithick
56038	CF	Western Mail
56040	CF	Oystermouth
56053	CF	Sir Morgannwg Ganol/County of Mid Glamorgan
56063	TO	Bardon Hill
56074	TO	Kellingley Colliery
56075	TO	West Yorkshire Enterprise
56095	TO	Harworth Colliery
56122	TO	Wilton-Coalpower
56123	TO	Drax Power Station
56124	TO	Blue Circle Cement
56131	TO	Ellington Colliery
56132	TO	Fina Energy
56133	TO	Crewe Locomotive Works
56134	TO	Blyth Power
56135	TO	Port of Tyne Authority

CLASS 58 B.R.E.L. TYPE 5 Co-Co

Built: 1983-87
Engine: Ruston-Paxman 3300 hp
Route Availability: 7
Maximum Tractive Effort: 61,800 lb
Transmission: Six Brush Traction Motors
Maximum Speed: 80 mph
Weight: 129 tonnes
Wheel Diameter: 3′ 8″

58001		TO	58006		TO	58011		TO	58016		TO
58002	●	TO	58007		TO	58012		TO	58017		TO
58003	●	TO	58008		TO	58013		TO	58018	●	TO
58004		TO	58009		TO	58014	●	TO	58019		TO
58005		TO	58010		TO	58015		TO	58020	●	TO

58021	TO	58029		TO	58037		TO	58045		TO
58022	TO	58030		TO	58038		TO	58046		TO
58023	TO	58031		TO	58039	•	TO	58047		TO
58024	TO	58032		TO	58040	•	TO	58048		TO
58025	TO	58033		TO	58041	•	TO	58049	•	TO
58026	TO	58034	•	TO	58042	•	TO	58050	•	TO
58027	TO	58035		TO	58043		TO			
58028	TO	58036		TO	58044		TO			

•

58002	TO	Daw Mill Colliery
58003	TO	Markham Colliery
58014	TO	Didcot Power Station
58018	TO	High Marnham Power Station
58020	TO	Doncaster Works
58034	TO	Bassetlaw
58039	TO	Rugeley Power Station
58040	TO	Cottam Power Station
58041	TO	Ratcliffe Power Station
58042	TO	Ironbridge Power Station
58049	TO	Littleton Colliery
58050	TO	Toton Traction Depot

CLASS 59 GENERAL MOTORS TYPE 5 Co-Co

Built: 1985 in USA
Maximum Speed: 60 mph
Engine: General Motors 3,300 hp
Weight: 126 tonnes
Route Availability: 7
Wheel Diamater: 3′ 4″
Maximum Tractive Effort: 122,000 lb
Transmission: General Motors D77B Traction Motors

59001	FYM	Yeoman Endeavour
59002	FYM	Yeoman Enterprise
59003	FYM	Yeoman Highlander
59004	FYM	Yeoman Challenger
59005 (on order)		

CLASS 60 BRUSH TYPE 5 Co-Co

Built: 1989 onwards
Engine: Mirrlees 3100 hp
Route Availability: 7
Maximum Tractive Effort: 106,500 lb
Transmission: Brush Traction Motors
Maximum Speed:
Weight: 126 tonnes
Wheel Diameter: 3′ 8″

60001	60014	60027	60040
60002	60015	60028	60041
60003	60016	60029	60042
60004	60017	60030	60043
60005	60018	60031	60044
60006	60019	60032	60045
60007	60020	60033	60046
60008	60021	60034	60047
60009	60022	60035	60048
60010	60023	60036	60049
60011	60024	60037	60050
60012	60025	60038	
60013	60026	60039	

BRITISH RAIL ELECTRIC LOCOMOTIVES

CLASS 73 BRITISH RAIL/ENGLISH ELECTRIC Bo-Bo ELECTRO-DIESEL

Built: 1962-67
Voltage: 660-750 V DC Third Rail
Engine: English Electric 600 hp
Wheel Diameter: 3′ 4″
Maximum Tractive Effort: 34,000-42,000 lb
Transmission: Four English Electric Traction Motors
Maximum Speed: 80-90 mph
Weight: 76-77 tonnes
Route Availability: 6

73/0

73001	SL	73004	SL	The Bluebell Railway
73002	SL	73005	SL	Mid-Hants,Watercress Line
73003	SL	73006	SL	

73/1

73101	●	SL
73103		SL
73104		SL
73105	●	SL
73106		SL
73107		SL
73108		SL
73109		SL
73110		SL
73111		SL
73112		SL
73114		SL
73117	●	SL
73118	●	SL
73119	●	SL
73126		SL
73128		SL
73129	●	SL
73130	●	SL
73131	●	SL
73132		SL
73133		SL
73134	●	SL
73135		SL
73136		SL
73138	●	SL
73139		SL
73140		SL
73141		SL
73201	●	SL
73202	●	SL
73203		SL
73204	●	SL
73205	●	SL
73206	●	SL
73207	●	SL
73208	●	SL
73209		SL
73210	●	SL
73211	●	SL
73212	●	SL

●

73101	SL	Brighton Evening Argus
73105	SL	Quadrant
73117	SL	University of Surrey
73118	SL	The Romney, Hythe and Dymchurch Railway
73119	SL	Kentish Mercury
73129	SL	City of Winchester
73130	SL	City of Portsmouth
73131	SL	County of Surrey
73134	SL	Woking Homes 1885-1985
73138	SL	Post Haste-150 Years of Travelling Post Offices
73201	SL	Broadlands
73202	SL	Royal Observer Corps
73204	SL	Stewarts Lane 1860-1985
73205	SL	London Chamber of Commerce
73206	SL	Gatwick Express
73207	SL	County of East Sussex
73208	SL	Croydon 1883-1983
73210	SL	Selhurst
73211	SL	County of West Sussex
73212	SL	Airtour Suisse

CLASS 81 BRITISH THOMSON HOUSTON Bo-Bo

Built: 1959-64
Voltage: 25 kV AC overhead
Transmission: Four AEI Traction Motors
Wheel Diameter: 4′ 0″
Maximum Speed: 80 mph
Weight: 79 tonnes
Route Availability: 6
Maximum Tractive Effort: 50,000 lb

81002	GW	81007	GW	81011	GW	81017	GW
81004	GW	81009	GW	81012	GW		
81005	GW	81010	GW	81013	GW		

CLASS 83 ENGLISH ELECTRIC Bo-Bo

Built: 1960-62
Voltage: 25 kV AC overhead
Wheel Diameter: 4′ 0″
Maximum Speed: 40 mph
Weight: 76 tonnes
Route Availability: 6
Transmission: Four English Electric Traction Motors
Maximum Tractive Effort: 38,000 lb

83009	WN	83012	WN

CLASS 85 BRITISH RAIL Bo-Bo

Built: 1961-64
Voltage: 25 kV AC overhead
Transmission: Four AEI Traction Motors
Wheel Diameter: 4′ 0″
Maximum Speed: 80/100 mph
Weight: 83 tonnes
Route Availability: 6
Maximum Tractive Effort: 50,000 lb

85002	CE	85013	CE	85025	CE	85034	CE
85003	CE	85014	CE	85026	CE	85035	CE
85004	CE	85015	CE	85028	CE	85036	CE
85005	CE	85016	CE	85030	CE	85037	CE
85006	CE	85018	CE	85031	CE	85038	CE
85007	CE	85019	CE	85032	CE	85040	CE
85008	CE	85020	CE				
85009	CE	85021	CE				
85010	CE	85022	CE				
85011	CE	85023	CE				
85012	CE	85024	CE				

CLASS 86 — BRITISH RAIL — Bo-Bo

Built: 1965-66
Maximum Speed: 100/110 mph
Voltage: 25 kV AC overhead
Weight: 83-87 tonnes
Transmission: Four AEI Traction Motors
Route Availability: 6
Wheel Diameter: 3′ 9″, 3′ 9½″
Maximum Tractive Effort: 46,500 lb – 58,000 lb

6/1 modified at Crewe with 87/0 motors and bogies.

86101	WN	Sir William A Stanier FRS
86102	WN	Robert A Riddles
86103	WN	Andre Chapelon

86/2 modified at Crewe with flexicoil springs and SAB resilient wheels.

86204	WN	City of Carlisle
86206	WN	City of Stoke on Trent
86207	WN	City of Lichfield
86208	WN	City of Chester
86209	WN	City of Coventry
86210	WN	City of Edinburgh
86212	WN	Preston Guild
86213	WN	Lancashire Witch
86214	WN	Sans Pareil
86215	WN	Joseph Chamberlain
86216	WN	Meteor
86218	WN	Planet
86219	WN	Phoenix
86220	WN	The Round Tabler
86221	WN	BBC Look East
86223	WN	Norwich Union
86224	WN	Caledonian
86225	WN	Hardwicke
86226	WN	Royal Mail Midlands
86227	WN	Sir Henry Johnson
86228	WN	Vulcan Heritage
86229	WN	Sir John Betjeman
86230	WN	The Duke of Wellington
86231	WN	Starlight Express
86232	WN	Harold Macmillan

86234	WN	J. B. Priestley OM
86235	WN	Novelty
86236	WN	Josiah Wedgwood Master Potter 1730-1795
86237	WN	Sir Charles Halle
86238	WN	European Community
86240	WN	Bishop Eric Treacy
86242	WN	James Kennedy G.C.
86243	WN	The Boys' Brigade
86244	WN	The Royal British Legion
86245	WN	Dudley Castle
86247	WN	Abraham Darby
86248	WN	Sir Clwyd/County of Clwyd
86249	WN	County of Merseyside
86250	WN	The Glasgow Herald
86251	WN	The Birmingham Post
86252	WN	The Liverpool Daily Post
86253	WN	The Manchester Guardian
86254	WN	William Webb Ellis
86255	WN	Penrith Beacon
86256	WN	Pebble Mill
86257	WN	Snowdon
86259	WN	Peter Pan
86260	WN	Driver Wallace Oakes G.C.
86261	WN	Driver John Axon G.C.

86/4 modified at Crewe from 86/0 and 86/3 fitted with flexicoil springs and resilient wheels.

86401	WN	
86402	WN	
86403	WN	
86404	WN	
86405	WN	
86406	WN	
86407	WN	The Institution of Electrical Engineers
86408	WN	St.John Ambulance
86409	WN	
86410	WN	
86411	WN	Airey Neave
86412	WN	Elizabeth Garrett Anderson
86413	WN	County of Lancashire
86414	WN	Frank Hornby
86415	WN	Rotary International

86416	WN	Wigan Pier
86417	WN	The Kingsman
86418	WN	
86419	WN	
86420	WN	
86421	WN	London School of Economics
86422	WN	
86423	WN	
86424	WN	
86425	WN	
86426	WN	
86427	WN	The Industrial Society
86428	WN	Aldaniti
86430	WN	Scottish National Orchestra
86431	WN	
86432	WN	Brookside
86433	WN	Wulfruna
86434	WN	University of London
86435	WN	
86436	WN	
86437	WN	
86438	WN	
86439	WN	

86/5 Modified at Crewe and fitted with tdm multiple working equipment

86501 (86258)	WN	Talyllyn-The First Preserved Railway
86502 (86222)	WN	Lloyd's List 250th.Anniversary
86503 (86205)	WN	City of Lancaster
86504 (86217)	WN	Halley's Comet
86505 (86246)	WN	Royal Anglian Regiment
86506 (86233)	WN	Laurence Olivier
86507 (86239)	WN	L.S.Lowry
86508 (86241)	WN	Glenfiddich
86509 (862)		
86510 (862)		

CLASS 87	BRITISH RAIL	Bo-Bo

Built: 1973-75 ***Maximum Speed:*** 110 mph
Voltage: 25 kV AC overhead ***Weight:*** 83 tonnes
Transmission: Four GEC Traction Motors ***Route Availability:*** 6
Wheel Diameter: 3′ 9 1/4″ ***Maximum Tractive Effort:*** 58,000 lb

87/0

87001	WN	Royal Scot
87002	WN	Royal Sovereign
87003	WN	Patriot
87004	WN	Britannia
87005	WN	City of London
87006	WN	Glasgow Garden Festival
87007	WN	City of Manchester
87008	WN	City of Liverpool
87009	WN	City of Birmingham
87010	WN	King Arthur
87011	WN	The Black Prince
87012	WN	The Royal Bank of Scotland
87013	WN	John O'Gaunt
87014	WN	Knight of the Thistle
87015	WN	Howard of Effingham
87016	WN	
87017	WN	Iron Duke
87018	WN	Lord Nelson
87019	WN	Sir Winston Churchill
87020	WN	North Briton
87021	WN	Robert the Bruce
87022	WN	Cock o'the North
87023	WN	Velocity
87024	WN	Lord of the Isles
87025	WN	County of Cheshire
87026	WN	Sir Richard Arkwright
87027	WN	Wolf of Badenoch
87028	WN	Lord President
87029	WN	Earl Marischal
87030	WN	Black Douglas
87031	WN	Hal o'the Wynd
87032	WN	Kenilworth
87033	WN	Thane of Fife
87034	WN	William Shakespeare
87035	WN	Robert Burns

87/1 Experimental Thyristor contolled loco.

87101 WN Stephenson

CLASS 89 BRUSH Co-Co

Built: 1986
Voltage: 25 kV AC overhead
Transmission:
Wheel Diameter: 3′ 9 1/4″
Maximum Speed: 125 mph
Weight: 105 tonnes
Route Availability: 6
Maximum Tractive Effort: 46,000 lb

89001 BN Avocet

CLASS 90 B.R.E.L./GENERAL ELECTRIC CO Bo-Bo

Built: 1987-onwards
Voltage: 25 kV AC overhead
Transmission: GEC Traction Motors
Wheel Diameter: 3′ 9 1/4″
Maximum Speed: 110 mph
Weight: 85 tonnes
Route Availability: 6
Maximum Tractive Effort: 43,100 lb

90001		WN	90014	WN	90027	90040
90002		WN	90015	WN	90028	90041
90003		WN	90016	WN	90029	90042
90004		WN	90017	WN	90030	90043
90005	●	WN	90018	WN	90031	90044
90006		WN	90019		90032	90045
90007		WN	90020		90033	90046
90008		WN	90021		90034	90047
90009		WN	90022		90035	90048
90010		WN	90023		90036	90049
90011	●	WN	90024		90037	90050
90012		WN	90025		90038	
90013		WN	90026		90039	

●

90005 WN Financial Times
90011 WN The Chartered Institute of Transport

CLASS 91 B.R.E.L./GENERAL ELECTRIC CO Bo-Bo

Built: 1988-onwards
Voltage: 25 kV AC overhead
Transmission: GEC Traction Motors
Wheel Diameter: 3′ 3$^1/_4$″
Maximum Speed: 125 mph
Weight: 82 tonnes
Route Availability: 7
Maximum Tractive Effort:

91001	BN	91009	BN	91017	91025
91002	BN	91010		91018	91026
91003	BN	91011		91019	91027
91004	BN	91012		91020	91028
91005	BN	91013		91021	91029
91006	BN	91014		91022	91030
91007	BN	91015		91023	91031
91008	BN	91016		91024	

DEPARTMENTAL LOCOMOTIVES

03179	R.C.E.Loco	RY
20001	Training Loco	TO
45121	Train Heating Test Loco RTC	
97204(31326)	Test Train Loco	RTC
97251(25305)	Ethel 2 Train Heating Unit	CL
97252(25314)	Ethel 3 Train Heating Unit	BY
97403(46035)	Ixion Test Train Loco	RTC
97404(46045)		Mickleover(u)
97472(47472)		CD
97480(47480)	Robin Hood	CD
97545(47545)		CD
97561(47561)		CD
97651(Pwm651)	P.W.Shunter	CF
97653(Pwm653)	P.W.Shunter	Radyr
97654(Pwm654)	P.W.Shunter	RG
97701(M61136)	Battery Loco	BD
97702(M61139)	Battery Loco	BD
97703(M61182)	Battery Loco	HE
97704(M61185)	Battery Loco	HE
97705(M61184)	Battery Loco	HE

97706(M61189)	Battery Loco	HE
97707(M61166)	Battery Loco	HE
97708(M61173)	Battery Loco	HE
97800(08600)	Ivor Depot Shunter	SG
97805(03079)	R.C.E.Loco	RY
97806(09017)	Severn Tunnel Emergency Loco	CF
ADB968021(84009)	Mobile Load Bank	CE
ADB968027(25912)	Tamworth Castle Training Loco	HO
ADB968028(27024)	Training Loco	ED

Note: 97805 retains its original number.

HIGH SPEED TRAINS

Trailer Buffet First (TRB)

40204	PM	40207	PM	40210	PM	40212	PM
40205	PM	40208	PM	40211	PM	40213	PM
40206	PM	40209	PM				

Trailer Buffet (Unclassified) (TRUB)

40322	LA	40324	LA	40326	LA	40331	LA
40323	LA	40325	LA	40327	LA	40355	LA

Trailer Buffet Standard (TRSB)

40401	PM	40418	OO	40425	PM	40432	LA
40402	PM	40419	LA	40426	LA	40433	LA
40403	PM	40420	PM	40427	OO	40434	LA
40414	PM	40421	PM	40428	PM	40435	PM
40415	PM	40422	PM	40429	NL	40436	OO
40416	OO	40423	OO	40430	PM	40437	OO
40417	OO	40424	OO	40431	LA		

Trailer Kitchen First (TRFK)

40501	NL	40505	HT	40511	HT	40513	BN

Trailer Modular Buffet First (TRFM)

40619 NL

Trailer Buffet First (TRFB)

40700	NL	40701	BN	40702	BN	40703	BN

40704	BN	40716	BN	40736	BN	40747	NL
40705	BN	40717	BN	40737	NL	40748	NL
40706	BN	40718	BN	40738	NL	40749	HT
40707	BN	40720	BN	40739	BN	40750	NL
40708	BN	40721	BN	40740	BN	40751	NL
40709	NL	40728	NL	40741	NL	40752	NL
40710	BN	40729	BN	40742	BN	40753	NL
40711	NL	40730	HT	40743	NL	40754	BN
40712	NL	40732	LA	40744	NL	40756	BN
40713	NL	40733	BN	40745	NL	40757	PM
40714	NL	40734	BN	40746	NL		
40715	BN	40735	NL				

Trailer First (TF)

41003	PM	41032	LA	41061	BN	41090	BN
41004	PM	41033	LA	41062	BN	41091	NL
41005	PM	41034	LA	41063	BN	41092	NL
41006	PM	41035	OO	41064	BN	41093	NL
41007	PM	41036	OO	41065	NL	41094	NL
41008	PM	41037	OO	41066	HT	41095	NL
41009	PM	41038	OO	41067	NL	41096	NL
41010	PM	41039	NL	41068	NL	41097	NL
41011	PM	41040	NL	41069	NL	41098	NL
41012	PM	41041	NL	41070	NL	41099	NL
41013	PM	41042	LA	41071	NL	41100	NL
41014	PM	41043	NL	41072	NL	41101	NL
41015	PM	41044	NL	41073	NL	41102	NL
41016	PM	41045	NL	41074	NL	41103	NL
41017	PM	41046	BN	41075	BN	41104	NL
41018	PM	41047	NL	41076	BN	41105	NL
41019	PM	41048	NL	41077	NL	41106	NL
41020	PM	41049	NL	41078	NL	41107	BN
41021	PM	41050	NL	41079	NL	41108	BN
41022	PM	41051	NL	41080	NL	41109	BN
41023	LA	41052	NL	41081	BN	41110	BN
41024	LA	41053	NL	41082	BN	41111	HT
41025	LA	41054	NL	41083	BN	41112	HT
41026	LA	41055	NL	41084	BN	41113	BN
41027	LA	41056	NL	41085	BN	41114	BN
41028	LA	41057	BN	41086	BN	41115	BN
41029	LA	41058	BN	41087	BN	41116	BN
41030	LA	41059	BN	41088	BN	41117	NL
41031	LA	41060	BN	41089	BN	41118	BN

41119	BN	41134	OO	41149	BN	41164	PM
41120	BN	41135	OO	41150	BN	41165	PM
41121	LA	41136	OO	41151	BN	41166	LA
41122	LA	41137	OO	41152	BN	41167	LA
41123	PM	41138	OO	41153	NL	41168	LA
41124	PM	41139	OO	41154	NL	41169	LA
41125	LA	41140	OO	41155	NL	41170	BN
41126	LA	41141	LA	41156	NL	41171	BN
41127	PM	41142	LA	41157	NL	41172	BN
41128	PM	41143	OO	41158	NL	41173	BN
41129	OO	41144	OO	41159	PM	41174	BN
41130	OO	41145	PM	41160	PM	41175	NL
41131	OO	41146	PM	41161	PM	41176	NL
41132	OO	41147	PM	41162	PM		
41133	OO	41148	PM	41163	PM		

Trailer Standard (TS)

42003	PM	42028	PM	42053	OO	42078	NL
42004	PM	42029	PM	42054	OO	42079	NL
42005	PM	42030	PM	42055	OO	42080	NL
42006	PM	42031	PM	42056	OO	42081	NL
42007	PM	42032	PM	42057	NL	42082	NL
42008	PM	42033	LA	42058	NL	42083	NL
42009	PM	42034	LA	42059	NL	42084	PM
42010	PM	42035	LA	42060	LA	42085	PM
42011	PM	42036	LA	42061	LA	42086	PM
42012	PM	42037	LA	42062	NL	42087	PM
42013	PM	42038	LA	42063	NL	42088	PM
42014	PM	42039	LA	42064	NL	42089	PM
42015	PM	42040	LA	42065	NL	42090	PM
42016	PM	42041	LA	42066	NL	42091	PM
42017	PM	42042	LA	42067	NL	42092	PM
42018	PM	42043	LA	42068	NL	42093	PM
42019	PM	42044	LA	42069	NL	42094	PM
42020	PM	42045	LA	42070	NL	42095	PM
42021	PM	42046	LA	42071	NL	42096	LA
42022	PM	42047	LA	42072	NL	42097	LA
42023	PM	42048	LA	42073	NL	42098	LA
42024	PM	42049	LA	42074	NL	42099	LA
42025	PM	42050	LA	42075	NL	42100	NL
42026	PM	42051	OO	42076	NL	42101	BN
42027	PM	42052	OO	42077	NL	42102	BN

42103	BN	42148	NL	42191	NL	42234	BN
42104	BN	42149	NL	42192	NL	42235	NL
42105	BN	42150	NL	42193	NL	42236	NL
42106	BN	42151	NL	42194	BN	42237	BN
42107	BN	42152	NL	42195	NL	42238	BN
42108	PM	42153	NL	42196	LA	42239	BN
42109	PM	42154	NL	42197	LA	42240	NL
42110	PM	42155	NL	42198	NL	42241	BN
42111	BN	42156	NL	42199	NL	42242	BN
42112	BN	42157	NL	42200	NL	42243	BN
42113	BN	42158	NL	42201	NL	42244	BN
42115	BN	42159	BN	42202	NL	42245	NL
42116	BN	42160	BN	42203	NL	42246	BN
42117	BN	42161	BN	42204	NL	42247	BN
42118	NL	42162	BN	42205	NL	42248	BN
42119	BN	42163	BN	42206	NL	42249	BN
42120	BN	42164	BN	42207	NL	42250	NL
42121	BN	42165	BN	42208	NL	42251	LA
42122	BN	42166	BN	42209	NL	42252	LA
42123	BN	42167	BN	42210	NL	42253	LA
42124	BN	42168	BN	42211	NL	42254	PM
42125	BN	42169	BN	42212	NL	42255	PM
42126	NL	42170	BN	42213	NL	42256	PM
42127	BN	42171	BN	42214	NL	42257	PM
42128	BN	42172	BN	42215	NL	42258	PM
42129	BN	42173	BN	42216	LA	42259	LA
42130	BN	42174	BN	42217	BN	42260	LA
42131	NL	42175	BN	42218	BN	42261	LA
42132	NL	42176	BN	42219	BN	42262	PM
42133	NL	42177	BN	42220	NL	42263	PM
42134	BN	42178	BN	42221	LA	42264	PM
42135	NL	42179	BN	42222	BN	42265	PM
42136	NL	42180	BN	42223	BN	42266	PM
42137	NL	42181	BN	42224	BN	42267	OO
42138	BN	42182	BN	42225	NL	42268	OO
42139	NL	42183	BN	42226	BN	42269	OO
42140	NL	42184	BN	42227	HT	42270	PM
42141	NL	42185	BN	42228	HT	42271	OO
42143	NL	42186	BN	42229	NL	42272	OO
42144	NL	42187	BN	42230	NL	42273	OO
42145	NL	42188	BN	42231	BN	42274	PM
42146	NL	42189	BN	42232	BN	42275	OO
42147	NL	42190	BN	42233	BN	42276	OO

42277	OO	42295	OO	42313	LA	42331	NL
42278	PM	42296	OO	42314	LA	42332	NL
42279	OO	42297	OO	42315	LA	42333	NL
42280	OO	42298	PM	42316	LA	42334	BN
42281	OO	42299	PM	42317	LA	42335	BN
42282	PM	42300	PM	42318	LA	42336	BN
42283	OO	42301	PM	42319	LA	42337	BN
42284	OO	42302	PM	42320	LA	42338	BN
42285	OO	42303	PM	42321	LA	42339	NL
42286	PM	42304	PM	42322	PM	42340	NL
42287	OO	42305	PM	42323	NL	42341	BN
42288	OO	42306	LA	42324	NL	42342	LA
42289	OO	42307	LA	42325	NL	42343	PM
42290	PM	42308	LA	42326	BN	42344	LA
42291	LA	42309	LA	42327	BN	42345	LA
42292	LA	42310	LA	42328	BN		
42293	LA	42311	LA	42329	NL		
42294	PM	42312	LA	42330	BN		

Driving Motor Brake (DMB) *modified to work with class 91

43002	OO	
43003	OO	
43004	OO	
43005	OO	
43006	OO	
43007	OO	
43008	LA	
43009	LA	
43010	LA	
43011	LA	
43012	LA	
43013 *	BN	
43014 *	BN	
43015	LA	
43016	LA	
43017	LA	HTV West
43018	PM	
43019	LA	City of Swansea/Dinas Abertawe
43020	LA	
43021	LA	
43022	LA	
43023	LA	

43024	LA	
43025	LA	
43026	LA	City of Westminster
43027	LA	Westminster Abbey
43028	LA	
43029	LA	
43030	PM	
43031	PM	
43032	PM	
43033	PM	
43034	PM	
43035	PM	
43036	PM	
43037	PM	
43038	NL	National Railway Museum The First Ten Years 1975-1985
43039	NL	
43040	EC	
43041	EC	
43042	EC	
43043	NL	
43044	NL	
43045	NL	The Grammer School Doncaster AD1350
43046	NL	
43047	NL	Rotherham Enterprise
43048	NL	
43049	NL	Neville Hill
43050	NL	
43051	NL	The Duke and Duchess of York
43052	NL	City of Peterborough
43053	NL	County of Humberside
43054	NL	
43055	NL	
43056	BN	University of Bradford
43057	BN	Bounds Green
43058	NL	
43059	NL	
43060	NL	County of Leicestershire
43061	NL	City of Lincoln
43062	BN	
43063	BN	
43064	NL	City of York
43065 *	BN	

43066	NL	
43067	EC	
43068 *	BN	
43069	EC	
43070	EC	
43071	EC	
43072	NL	
43073	NL	
43074	BN	
43075	BN	
43076	NL	
43077	NL	County of Nottingham
43078	EC	Shildon,County Durham
43079	EC	
43080	BN	
43081	BN	
43082	BN	
43083	BN	
43084 *	BN	County of Derbyshire
43085 *	BN	City of Bradford
43086	EC	
43087	EC	
43088	EC	XIII Commonwealth Games Scotland 1986
43089	EC	
43090	EC	
43091	EC	Edinburgh Military Tattoo
43092	EC	Highland Chieftain
43093	EC	York Festival 88
43094	EC	
43095 *	HT	Heaton
43096	HT	The Queen's Own Hussars
43097	HT	The Light Infantry
43098	HT	Tyne and Wear Metropolitan County
43099	HT	
43100	EC	Craigentinny
43101	EC	Edinburgh International Festival
43102	HT	City of Wakefield
43103	HT	John Wesley
43104	HT	County of Cleveland
43105	HT	Hartlepool
43106 *	BN	
43107 *	BN	
43108	NL	

43109	NL	
43110	HT	Darlington
43111	NL	
43112	NL	
43113	HT	City of Newcastle upon Tyne
43114	BN	
43115	BN	
43116	NL	City of Kingston upon Hull
43117	NL	
43118	NL	Charles Wesley
43119	NL	
43120	NL	
43121	NL	West Yorkshire Metropolitan County
43122	NL	South Yorkshire Metropolitan County
43123 *	BN	
43124	PM	BBC Points West
43125	PM	Merchant Venturer
43126	PM	City of Bristol
43127	PM	
43128	PM	
43129	PM	
43130	PM	
43131	PM	Sir Felix Pole
43132	PM	Worshipful Company of Carmen
43133	PM	
43134	PM	
43135	PM	
43136	PM	
43137	PM	
43138 *	PM	
43139	OO	
43140	OO	
43141	OO	
43142	OO	
43143	OO	
43144	OO	
43145	OO	
43146	OO	
43147	OO	Red Cross
43148	OO	
43149	PM	BBC Wales Today
43150	PM	Bristol Evening Post
43151	PM	Blue Peter II

43152	NL	St.Peter's School York AD627
43153	NL	University of Durham
43154	NL	
43155	NL	BBC Look North
43156	NL	
43157	NL	Yorkshire Evening Post
43158	NL	
43159	NL	
43160	NL	
43161	NL	
43162	NL	Borough of Stevenage
43163	LA	
43164	NL	
43165	NL	
43166	LA	
43167	PM	
43168	PM	
43169	PM	
43170	PM	
43171	PM	
43172	PM	
43173	PM	
43174	PM	
43175	PM	
43176	PM	
43177	LA	
43178	LA	
43179	LA	
43180	OO	
43181	LA	
43182	LA	
43183	LA	
43184	LA	
43185	LA	
43186	LA	Sir Francis Drake
43187	LA	
43188	LA	
43189	LA	
43190	LA	
43191	LA	Seahawk
43192	LA	City of Truro
43193	NL	Yorkshire Post
43194	NL	Royal Signals
43195	NL	
43196	NL	The Newspaper Society
43197	NL	
43198	NL	

Class 08: No.08644 *Ponsandane* in InterCity 'Swallow' livery, seen at Penzance (PZ) on 20th August 1988.

(John S. Whiteley)

Class 08: No.08720 resplendent in Provincial sector livery, depicted at Haymarket depot (HA) on 29th May 1988.

(Brian Morrison)

Class 31: No.31400 is a new addition to the 31/4 class (ETH fitted), being a rebuild of No.31161. Photographed at Old Oak Common depot (OC) on 2nd July 1988.
(Michael J. Collins)

Class 33: No.33206 displayed at the Woking 150 exhibition on 29th May 1988 in Railfreight Speedlink Distribution sub-sector livery.
(Peter Nicholson)

Class 37: No.37401 *Mary Queen of Scots* was the first of the class to receive the InterCity livery. Seen at Crianlarich with the 07.00 Mallaig-Glasgow Queen St. on 31st August 1988.

(Brian Denton)

Class 47: No.47319 is named *Norsk Hydro* at Immingham on 3rd March 1988.

(Les Nixon)

Class 50: No.50149 heads a short ECC china clay train from Heathfield to Tavistock Junction Yard, 28th July 1988.

(Hugh Ballantyne)

Class 56: Ten members of the class at Knottingley depot (KY) on 14th May 1988, including Nos 56009/66/37/30/04/100/102.

(Les Nixon)

Class 59: No.59001 *Yeoman Endeavour* in the strange surroundings of the Severn Valley Railway, 7th May 1988.

(Gavin Morrison)

Class 90: No.90003 at Willesden depot (WN) on 18th June 1988.

(Michael J. Collins)

Class 91: No.91003 at Derby RTC Yard on 19th May 1988, together with Class 90 No.90008 and Class 89 No.89001.

(Colin J. Marsden)

Class 155: Set No.155318 (coach Nos 52318 + 57318) at Cardiff Central station on arrival from Birmingham, 16th February 1988.

(Hugh Ballantyne)

Class 319: No.319033 at St Pancras station on 12th July 1988.
(Brian Morrison)

Class 442: A "Wessex Electric" snakes out of Waterloo station, forming the 17.15 to Weymouth on 31st August 1988.
(John S. Whiteley)

Class 485 (5-VEC): No.485 041 at Brading, Isle of Wight on the 14.58 Ryde Pier Head-Shanklin, 1st June 1988.

(John Tuffs)

Track recording train, Nos DB999600 + DB999601 at Leicester on 12th May 1988.

(Brian Denton)

Trailer Guard's Standard (TGS)

44000	PM
44001	PM
44002	PM
44003	PM
44004	PM
44005	PM
44006	PM
44007	PM
44008	PM
44009	PM
44010	PM
44011	LA
44012	LA
44013	LA
44014	LA
44015	LA
44016	LA
44017	OO
44018	OO
44019	NL
44020	LA
44021	NL
44022	NL
44023	NL
44024	NL
44025	NL
44026	NL
44027	NL
44028	LA
44029	PM
44030	LA
44031	PM
44032	OO
44033	OO
44034	OO
44035	OO
44036	OO
44037	OO
44038	LA
44039	OO
44040	PM
44041	BN
44042	BN
44043	BN
44044	BN
44045	BN
44046	NL
44047	NL
44048	NL
44049	NL
44050	BN
44051	NL
44052	NL
44053	BN
44054	BN
44055	BN
44056	BN
44057	BN
44058	BN
44059	BN
44060	BN
44061	NL
44062	PM
44063	NL
44064	NL
44065	PM
44066	NL
44067	NL
44068	PM
44069	PM
44070	BN
44071	BN
44072	PM
44073	HT
44074	BN
44075	BN
44076	PM
44077	BN
44078	BN
44079	BN
44080	BN
44081	PM
44083	NL
44084	LA
44085	NL
44086	NL
44087	PM
44088	LA
44089	LA
44090	LA
44091	LA
44093	BN
44094	NL
44097	HT
44098	BN
44099	OO
44100	NL
44101	BN

BRITISH RAIL DIESEL MULTIPLE UNITS

Class 119 DMBC Gloucester R.C.& W.Co."Cross Country"

51057	CH	51066	RG	51074	RG
51060	RG	51071	CH	51076	RG
51062	RG	51073	RG	51079	RG
51065	RG				

Class 119 DMSL Gloucester R.C.& W.Co."Cross Country"

51086	RG	51095	CH	51103	RG
51088	RG	51099	RG	51104	RG
51090	RG	51101	CH	51107	RG
51094	RG				

Class 116 DMBS Derby"Suburban"

51128	CF	51131	TS	51134	CF	51138	TS
51129	TS	51132	CF	51135	CF	51139	CF
51130	TS	51133	TS	51136	TS	51140	CF

Class 116 DMS Derby"Suburban"

51141	CF	51144	TS	51147	CF	51151	TS
51142	TS	51145	CF	51148	CF	51152	CF
51143	TS	51146	TS	51149	TS	51153	CF

Class 101 DMBS Metro-Cammell

51174	HA	51185	NC	51203	HT	51216	HT
51175	NL	51187	NC	51205	LA	51217	HT
51177	NC	51188	NC	51206	NH	51218	NC
51178	NC	51189	NC	51207	CA	51219	LA
51179	LA	51190	RG	51208	CA	51220	OO
51180	NC	51191	NC	51210	HA	51221	OO
51181	LA	51192	NC	51211	RG	51222	CF
51182	HA	51194	NC	51212	OO	51223	LA
51183	NL	51197	HT	51213	NC	51224	ED
51184	NC	51201	NC	51215	NL	51225	OO

51226	RG	51231	HA	51244	HA	51249	ED
51227	NH	51234	HA	51245	HA	51252	NC
51228	HA	51241	HA	51246	LA	51253	HA
51230	NC	51243	NH	51247	NC		

Class 118 DMBS Birmingham R.C.& W.Co."Suburban"

51305	LA	51307	CF	51312	CF	51315	CF
51306	TS	51310	CF	51314	TS	51316	TS

Class 118 DMS Birmingham R.C.& W.Co."Suburban"

51319	OO	51321	TS	51327	CF	51330	CF
51320	LA	51325	CF	51329	TS	51331	TS

Class 117 DMBS Pressed Steel "Suburban"

51332	RG	51343	RG	51354	RG	51366	RG
51333	RG	51344	RG	51355	RG	51367	RG
51334	TS	51345	RG	51356	RG	51368	TS
51335	RG	51346	RG	51358	RG	51369	TS
51336	RG	51347	RG	51359	RG	51370	TS
51337	RG	51348	TS	51360	TS	51371	TS
51338	TS	51349	RG	51361	RG	51372	TS
51339	TS	51350	RG	51362	RG	51373	TS
51340	RG	51351	RG	51363	RG		
51341	RG	51352	TS	51364	TS		
51342	RG	51353	TS	51365	TS		

Class 117 DMS Pressed Steel "Suburban"

51374	RG	51385	RG	51396	RG	51408	RG
51375	RG	51386	RG	51397	RG	51409	RG
51376	TS	51387	RG	51398	RG	51410	TS
51377	RG	51388	RG	51399	RG	51411	TS
51378	RG	51389	RG	51400	RG	51412	TS
51379	RG	51390	TS	51401	RG	51413	TS
51380	TS	51391	RG	51402	TS	51414	TS
51381	RG	51392	RG	51404	RG	51415	TS
51382	TS	51393	RG	51405	RG		
51383	RG	51394	TS	51406	TS		
51384	RG	51395	TS	51407	TS		

Class 108 DMBS Derby "Lightweight"

51416	CF	51418	CH	51420	NH	51422	CH
51417	CH	51419	CH	51421	CH	51424	CH

Class 101 DMBS Metro-Cammell

51425	RG	51434	RG	51443	OO	51456	NH
51426	HA	51435	NH	51444	CA	51458	HT
51427	NC	51436	NL	51445	NL	51462	LE
51428	NC	51437	RG	51446	NL	51463	NL
51429	NC	51438	CA	51449	NH	51465	NL
51430 p	CA	51439 p	CA	51450	NL	51467	HT
51431	RG	51441 p	CA	51454	NL	51468	ED
51432	RG	51442	NC	51455	NL		

Class 101 DMCL Metro-Cammell

51495	NL	51505	CF	51515	HT	51524	NL
51496	HA	51506	NC	51516	HT	51529	NL
51498	RG	51508	NC	51517	NL	51530	LA
51499	RG	51509	CF	51519	NL	51531	HA
51500	NL	51510	NL	51520	NH	51532	NH
51501	RG	51511	LE	51521	HT	51533	NL
51503	RG	51512	NL	51522	HT	51538	NL
51504	RG	51513	CF	51523	NH		

Class 108 DMCL Derby "Lightweight"

51561	LE	51566	HA	51570	LA
51562	LE	51567	LE	51571	BY
51563	LE	51568	BX	51572	BY
51565	LE	51569	BX		

Class 115 DMBS Derby "Suburban"

51651	BY	51657	BY	51663	BY	51669	BY
51652	BY	51658	BY	51664	BY	51670	BY
51653	BY	51659	BY	51665	BY	51671	BY
51654	BY	51660	BY	51666	BY	51673	BY
51655	BY	51661	BY	51667	BY	51674	BY
51656	BY	51662	TS	51668	BY	51675	BY

51676	BY	51678	BY	51680	BY
51677	BY	51679	BY		

Class 101 DMBS Metro-Cammell

51795	NL	51800	HA
51798	NH	51801	NL
51799	NL		

Class 101 DMCL Metro-Cammell

51803	ED
51804	NL
51808	NL

Class 110 DMBC Birmingham RC&W "Calder Valley"

51809	NL	51817	NL	51828	NL
51812	NL	51823	NL		
51813	NL	51827	NL		

Class 110 DMCL Birmingham RC&W "Calder Valley"

51829	NL	51834	NL	51840	NL	51843	NL
51830	NL	51835	NL	51842	NL	51847	NL

Class 115 DMBS Derby "Suburban"

51849	BY	51863	BY	51876	TS	51890	BY
51851	TS	51865	TS	51877	TS	51891	BY
51852	TS	51866	BY	51878	BY	51892	TS
51853	TS	51867	TS	51879	BY	51893	BY
51854	TS	51868	TS	51880	TS	51894	BY
51855	BY	51869	TS	51883	BY	51895	BY
51856	TS	51870	TS	51884	TS	51896	BY
51857	BY	51871	BY	51885	BY	51897	TS
51858	TS	51872	BY	51886	BY	51898	TS
51859	TS	51873	BY	51887	BY	51899	BY
51860	TS	51874	BY	51888	BY	51900	BY
51862	TS	51875	BY	51889	BY		

51899 BY Aylesbury College Silver Jubilee 1987

Class 108 DMBS Derby "Lightweight"

51901	CH	51912	BY	51926	HA	51938	BX
51902	CH	51913	CH	51927	CH	51939	LA
51903	CH	51914	BY	51928	LE	51940	LA
51904	CH	51916	BY	51930	LE	51941	BX
51905	CH	51917	CH	51931	LE	51942	BY
51906	CH	51919	LE	51932	LA	51943	BX
51907	CH	51920	CH	51933	LA	51945	BX
51908	CH	51922	LE	51935	BX	51947	BX
51909	BY	51924	LE	51936	HA	51948	BX
51911	CH	51925	HA	51937	TS	51950	BX

Class 107 DMBS Derby "Heavyweight"

51985	HA	51991	HA	51998	ED	52006	ED
51986	ED	51992	HA	51999	ED	52007	ED
51987	ED	51993	ED	52000	HA	52008	ED
51988	HA	51994	HA	52001	ED	52010	ED
51989	ED	51996	ED	52004	ED		
51990	ED	51997	ED	52005	ED		

Class 107 DMCL Derby "Heavyweight"

52011	HA	52019	ED	52026	HA	52034	ED
52012	ED	52020	ED	52028	HA	52035	HA
52013	HA	52021	ED	52029	ED	52036	HA
52015	ED	52023	ED	52030	ED		
52016	ED	52024	ED	52031	ED		
52018	ED	52025	ED	52033	ED		

Class 108 DMCL Derby "Lightweight"

52038	LE	52048	LE	52058	BX
52039	BX	52049	BX	52059	HA
52041	LE	52050	BX	52060	BX
52042	HA	52051	HA	52061	LE
52043	HA	52053	HA	52062	BX
52044	LE	52054	LA	52063	LA
52045	LE	52055	LE	52064	BX
52046	LE	52056	BX	52065	BX
52047	LA	52057	LA		

Class 110 DMBC Birmingham RC&W "Calder Valley"

52066	NL	52069	NL	52072	NL
52067	NL	52071	NL	52075	NL

Class 110 DMCL Birmingham RC&W "Calder Valley"

52077	NL	52081	NL	52084	NL
52080	NL	52082	NL	52085	NL

Class 150/1 DMSL BREL Sprinter (150101-150150)

52101	DY	52114	DY	52127	DY	52140	DY
52102	DY	52115	DY	52128	DY	52141	DY
52103	DY	52116	DY	52129	DY	52142	DY
52104	DY	52117	DY	52130	DY	52143	DY
52105	DY	52118	DY	52131	DY	52144	DY
52106	DY	52119	DY	52132	DY	52145	DY
52107	DY	52120	DY	52133	DY	52146	DY
52108	DY	52121	DY	52134	DY	52147	DY
52109	DY	52122	DY	52135	DY	52148	DY
52110	DY	52123	DY	52136	DY	52149	DY
52111	DY	52124	DY	52137	DY	52150	DY
52112	DY	52125	DY	52138	DY		
52113	DY	52126	DY	52139	DY		

Class 150/2 DMSL BREL Sprinter (150201-150285)

52201	NH	52216	NL	52231	NH	52246	NL
52202	NL	52217	NH	52232	NL	52247	CF
52203	NH	52218	NL	52233	NH	52248	NL
52204	NL	52219	NH	52234	NL	52249	CF
52205	DY	52220	NL	52235	NH	52250	NL
52206	NL	52221	NH	52236	NL	52251	CF
52207	NH	52222	NL	52237	NH	52252	NL
52208	HA	52223	NH	52238	NL	52253	DY
52209	NH	52224	NL	52239	NH	52254	NL
52210	NL	52225	NH	52240	NL	52255	HA
52211	NH	52226	NL	52241	NH	52256	NL
52212	NL	52227	NH	52242	NL	52257	HA
52213	NH	52228	NL	52243	NH	52258	NL
52214	NL	52229	NH	52244	NL	52259	HA
52215	NH	52230	NL	52245	HA	52260	NL

52261	CF
52262	NL
52263	CF
52264	HA
52265	CF
52266	CF
52267	CF
52268	CF
52269	CF
52270	CF
52271	CF
52272	CF
52273	CF
52274	CF
52275	CF
52276	CF
52277	CF
52278	CF
52279	CF
52280	CF
52281	CF
52282	CF
52283	HA
52284	HA
52285	HA

Class 155 DMSL Leyland Super Sprinter (155301-155347)

52301	CF
52302	CF
52303	CF
52304	CF
52305	CF
52306	CF
52307	CF
52308	CF
52309	CF
52310	CF
52311	CF
52312	CF
52313	CF
52314	CF
52315	CF
52316	CF
52317	CF
52318	CF
52319	CF
52320	CF
52321	CF
52322	CF
52323	CF
52324	CF
52325	CF
52326	CF
52327	CF
52328	CF
52329	CF
52330	CF
52331	CF
52332	CF
52333	CF
52334	CF
52335	CF
52341	NL
52342	NL
52343	NL
52344	NL
52345	NL
52346	NL
52347	NL

Class 156 DMSL Metro-Cammell Super Sprinter (156401-156514)

52401	NC
52402	NC
52403	NC
52404	NC
52405	NC
52406	NC
52407	NC
52408	NC
52409	NC
52410	NC
52411	NC
52412	NC
52413	NC
52414	NC
52415	NC
52416	NC
52417	NC
52418	NC
52419	NC
52420	NC
52421	NC
52422	NC
52423	NC
52424	NC
52425	NC
52426	NC
52427	NC
52428	NC
52429	NC
52430	CK
52431	CK
52432	CK
52433	CK
52434	CK
52435	CK
52436	CK
52437	CK
52438	NC
52439	CK
52440	NC
52441	NL
52442	CK
52443	NL
52444	NL
52445	IS
52446	IS
52447	IS
52448	IS
52449	IS
52450	IS
52451	IS
52452	IS
52453	IS
52454	IS
52455	IS
52456	HA
52457	HA
52458	HA
52459	HA
52460	HA
52461	HA
52462	
52463	
52464	
52465	
52466	
52467	
52468	
52469	
52470	
52471	
52472	
52473	
52474	
52475	
52476	

52477
52478
52479
52480
52481
52482
52483
52484
52485
52486
52487
52488
52489
52490
52491
52492
52493
52494
52495
52496
52497
52498
52499
52500
52501
52502
52503
52504
52505
52506
52507
52508
52509
52510
52511
52512
52513
52514

Class 158 DMSL Super Sprinter (158701-158797)

52701
52702
52703
52704
52705
52706
52707
52708
52709
52710
52711
52712
52713
52714
52715
52716
52717
52718
52719
52720
52721
52722
52723
52724
52725
52726
52727
52728
52729
52730
52731
52732
52733
52734
52735
52736
52737
52738
52739
52740
52741
52742
52743
52744
52745
52746
52747
52748
52749
52750
52751
52752
52753
52754
52755
52756
52757
52758
52759
52760
52761
52762
52763
52764
52765
52766
52767
52768
52769
52770
52771
52772
52773
52774
52775
52776
52777
52778
52779
52780
52781
52782
52783
52784
52785
52786
52787
52788
52789
52790
52791
52792
52793
52794
52795
52796
52797
52798
52799
52800
52801
52802
52803
52804
52805
52806
52807
52808

Class 114 DMBS Derby "Heavyweight"

53002	TS	53015	TS	53026	TS	53037	TS
53004 p	CA	53018	TS	53027 p	TS	53038 p	CA
53005	TS	53019	TS	53030	TS	53039	TS
53006	TS	53020 p	CA	53035 p	CA	53044	TS
53008	TS	53021	TS	53036	TS	53046 p	CA

Class 116 DMBS Derby "Suburban"

53050	TS	53058	TS	53079	TS	53089	CF
53053	TS	53060	TS	53080	CF	53090	TS
53054	TS	53061	TS	53082	TS		
53055	TS	53071	TS	53083	OO		
53056	TS	53073	TS	53086	CF		

Class 116 DMS Derby "Suburban"

53092	TS	53102	TS	53116	TS	53128	CF
53093	TS	53106	TS	53122	CF	53131	CF
53101	TS	53114	TS	53124	TS	53132	TS

Class 101 DMCL Metro-Cammell

53139	NC	53146	ED	53150	NC
53141	NL	53149	NC		

Class 101 DMBS Metro-Cammell

53155	OO
53157	LA

Class 101 DMCL Metro-Cammell

53158	ED	53160	ED	53163	HA
53159	NL	53162	NL		

Class 101 DMBS Metro-Cammell

53164	HA
53165	LA

Class 101 DMCL Metro-Cammell

53168	NC	53177	NC	53186	HA	53194	ED
53169	NH	53180	NC	53187	HA	53195	HT
53170	NC	53181	NC	53188	HT	53196	HT
53171	HA	53182	HT	53189	HA	53197	HA
53176	HA	53185	ED	53193	NC		

Class 101 DMBS Metro-Cammell

53198	HA	53208	NC	53219	NH	53230 p	CA
53200	LA	53211	HA	53221 p	CA	53231	NC
53201	NC	53212	LA	53222	CH	53233 p	CA
53202	NC	53214	NL	53223	LA		
53203	NC	53215	HA	53224	CF		
53204	NC	53216	HA	53228	NC		
53207	OO	53218 p	CA	53229	HT		

Class 101 DMCL Metro-Cammell

53235	NH	53239	HA	53242	HA	53244	HA
53237	NL	53240	NH	53243	HA	53245	HA
53238	NC	53241	ED				

Class 101 DMBS Metro-Cammell

53247	LA	53250	HA	53253	HA	53256	LA
53248	LA	53251	NH	53255 p	CA	53257	HT

Class 101 DMCL Metro-Cammell

53260	HA	53264	NH	53266	NC	53268	HA
53263	CH	53265	RG	53267	NC	53269	HA

Class 101 DMBS Metro-Cammell

53290	HA	53305	NC	53311	RG	53317	CH
53291	HA	53306	CH	53312	RG	53318	CH
53293	NC	53307	CH	53314	RG	53319	CF
53294	HA	53308	RG	53315	LA		
53296	OO	53309	CH				
53303	CH	53310	RG				

Class 101 DMCL Metro-Cammell

53321	NC	53325	CH	53331	RG	53335	NL
53322	RG	53326	RG	53332	RG	53336	CH
53323	CH	53327	RG	53333	RG	53337	CH
53324	CH	53330	LA	53334	NH	53338	CH

Class 100 DMBS Gloucester RC&W

53355 NH

Class 105 DMBS Cravens

53361 p	CA	53365 p	CA	53368 p	CA
53364 p	CA	53367 p	CA	53373 p	CA

Class 104 DMBS Birmingham RC&W

53421 NH

Class 104 DMCL Birmingham RC&W

53425 NH
53427 NH

Class 104 DMBS Birmingham RC&W

53429	OO	53444	NH	53464	NH	53474	NHu
53431	NH	53447	NH	53465	NH	53476	NH
53437	OO	53451	NH	53466	NH	53477	OO
53439	NH	53454	NH	53468	NH	53478	ED
53442	NH	53455	OO	53470	OO	53479	OO
53443	NH	53460	NHu	53472	HA		

Class 104 DMCL Birmingham RC&W

53487	NH	53501	NHu	53518	NH
53492	NH	53504	NH	53520	NH
53493	NH	53507	NH	53522	NH
53494	NH	53511	NH	53528	NH
53496	NHu	53512	NH	53529	NH
53499	NH	53516	NH	53530	ED
53500	NH	53517	NH	53531	NH

Class 104 DMBS Birmingham RC&W

53532	NH	53536	NH	53540	OO
53534	NH	53539	OO	53541	NH

Class 104 DMCL Birmingham RC&W

53556 NH

Class 108 DMBS Derby "Lightweight"

53599	BY	53612	BR	53620	BR	53627	CF
53601	NL	53614	BR	53621	BR	53628	BY
53602	BR	53616	BR	53622	BR	53629	CF
53606	NH	53617	CF	53624	CF		
53607	NL	53618	BR	53625	LE		
53608	BR	53619	BR	53626	BX		

Class 108 DMCL Derby "Lightweight"

53630	HA	53634	BX	53638	LA	53643	HA
53631	HA	53635	CF	53639	LA	53644	HA
53632	NL	53636	BX	53641	HA	53645	HA
53633	LE	53637	LA	53642	NL	53646	LA

Class 120 DMSL Swindon "Cross-Country"

53658	HA
53682	HA
53686	HA

Class 120 DMBC Swindon "Cross-Country"

53699	HA
53700	HA
53732	HA
53733	HA

Class 101 DMCL Metro-Cammell

53746	HT
53751	RG

Class 105 DMCL Cravens

53812	NH

Class 116 DMBS Derby"Suburban"

53818	TS	53837	TS	53849	TS	53858	CF
53820	OO	53838	TS	53850	TS	53863	TS
53822	TS	53843	CF	53853	TS	53865	TS
53826	TS	53844	TS	53854	TS	53866	NH
53827	TS	53848	CF	53855	CF	53869	NH

Class 116 DMS Derby "Suburban"

53873	TS	53887	NH	53897	TS	53916	TS
53878	TS	53890	TS	53902	TS	53919	TS
53880	TS	53891	TS	53907	TS	53921	TS
53881	TS	53893	TS	53908	CF	53922	NH
53886	TS	53894	TS	53911	CF		

Class 108 DMBS Derby "Lightweight"

53924	CH	53941	BR	53956	HT	53973	HT
53925	BX	53942	LE	53957	HT	53974	NH
53926	LE	53943	NH	53958	HT	53975	NH
53927	NH	53944	NH	53959	HT	53976	NH
53928	LE	53945	LE	53960	HT	53977	NH
53930	BX	53947	LE	53962	HT	53978	NH
53931	CH	53948	NH	53963	HT	53980	NH
53932	BX	53949	NH	53964	CH	53981	NH
53933	HA	53950	HT	53965	CH	53982	NH
53934	NH	53951	HT	53966	CH	53983	NH
53935	LE	53952	HT	53968	CH	53986	CH
53938	CH	53953	HT	53969	CH	53987	CH
53939	LE	53954	HT	53970	NH		
53940	CH	53955	HT	53971	NH		

Class 114 DTCL Derby"Heavyweight"

54006	TS	54010	TS	54013	TS	54024	TS
54008	TS	54011	TS	54015	TS	54026 p	CA
54009	TS	54012	TS	54019	TS	54027	TS

54028 p	CA	54041 p	CA	54043	TS
54039	TS	54042 p	CA	54047	TS

Class 101 DTCL Metro-Cammell

54050	NC	54061	NH	54071	NHu	54085	NH
54054	CHu	54062	NC	54073	NC	54091	CH
54055	NC	54065	NC	54075	NH		
54056	NH	54068	CA	54080	NC		
54060	NC	54070	OO	54081	TS		

Class 104 DTCL Birmingham RC&W

54179	RG

Class 108 DTCL Derby "Lightweight"

54191	BR	54201	BR	54205	BR	54210	CF
54194	BY	54202	BR	54207	BR	54212	CH
54196	NH	54203	BR	54208	BR	54213	BY
54197	BR	54204	BR	54209	BR	54214	CH

Class 101 DTCL Metro-Cammell

54218	NC
54219	NHu
54220	NH

Class 108 DTCL Derby "Lightweight"

54221	CH	54239	HT	54253	NH	54268	NH
54222	BY	54240	HT	54256	NH	54269	CH
54223	BY	54241	HT	54257	BY	54270	CH
54224	BY	54242	HT	54258	NH	54271	BY
54225	NH	54243	HT	54259	BY	54272	CH
54227	HT	54244	HT	54260	CH	54273	CH
54228	BY	54245	HT	54261	NH	54274	BY
54230	BR	54246	NH	54262	HT	54275	CH
54231	CH	54247	CH	54263	HT	54276	CH
54232	CH	54248	CH	54264	NH	54277	CH
54235	HT	54249	CH	54265	HT	54278	CH
54236	HT	54251	CH	54266	NH	54279	BY
54238	HT	54252	CH	54267	CF		

Class 121 DTSL Pressed Steel "Suburban"

54280	OO	54287	OO
54283	OO	54289	OO
54284	LA		

Class 101 DTCL Metro-Cammell

54332	NC	54352	NC	54371	OO	54393	NC
54335	NC	54354	NC	54372	OO	54396	OO
54340	NC	54355	NC	54375	NHu	54398	NHu
54342	NC	54358	BY	54379	NC	54399	NC
54343	NC	54362	NH	54380	NC	54401	TSu
54345	HTu	54363	NC	54381	NHu	54402	CA
54346	NC	54365	NL	54382	CA	54405	NC
54347	NC	54367	ED	54385	OO	54408	NH
54348	NC	54368	NC	54387	NC		
54350	CHu	54369	NC	54388	NC		
54351	NC	54370	HTu	54391	HTu		

Class 108 DTCL Derby "Lightweight"

54484	CH	54489	CH	54494	CH	54499	BY
54485	CH	54490	CH	54495	BY	54500	BY
54486	CH	54491	BY	54496	CH	54501	CH
54487	CH	54492	BR	54497	CH	54503	NH
54488	CH	54493	BY	54498	CH	54504	NH

Class 114 DTPMV Derby"Heavyweight"Parcels

54900	CA
54901	CA
54902	CA

Class 122 DMBS Gloucester"Suburban"

55000	LA	55004	BY	55006	LA	55011	BY
55003	LA	55005	LA	55009	LA	55012	LA

Class 121 DMBS Pressed Steel "Suburban"

55020	OO	55021	OO	55022	OO	55023	OO

55024	OO	55027	OO	55030	OO	55033	TS
55025	OO	55028	OO	55031	OO	55034	TS
55026	LA	55029	OO	55032	TS		

Class 150/0 DMSL BREL Prototype Sprinter (150001)

55200 DY

Class 154 DMSL BREL Super Sprinter (154002)

55201 DY

Class 151 DMSL Metro-Cammell Prototype (151003/4)

55202 DY
55203 DY

Class 150/0 DMS BREL Prototype Sprinter (150001)

55300 DY

Class 154 DMS BREL Super Sprinter (154002)

55301 DY

Class 151 DMS Metro-Cammell Prototype (151003/4)

55302 DY
55303 DY

Class 150/0 MS BREL Prototype Sprinter (150001)

55400 DY

Class 154 MS BREL Super Sprinter (154002)

55401 DY

Class 151 MS Metro-Cammell Prototype (151003/4)

55402 DY
55403 DY

Class 140 DMS Prototype Railbus (140001)

55500 NL

Class 140 DMSL Prototype Railbus (140001)

55501 NL

Class 141 DMS Leyland/BREL Railbus (141102-141120/141101 on refurbishment)

55502	NLu	55507	NL	55512	NL	55517	NL
55503	NL	55508	NL	55513	NL	55518	NL
55504	NL	55509	NL	55514	NL	55519	NL
55505	NL	55510	NL	55515	NL	55520	NL
55506	NL	55511	NL	55516	NL	55521	NL

Class 141 DMSL Leyland/BREL Railbus (141102-141120/141101 on refurbishment)

55522	NLu	55527	NL	55532	NL	55537	NL
55523	NL	55528	NL	55533	NL	55538	NL
55524	NL	55529	NL	55534	NL	55539	NL
55525	NL	55530	NL	55535	NL	55540	NL
55526	NL	55531	NL	55536	NL	55541	NL

Class 142 DMS Leyland/BREL Railbus (142001-142050)

55542	NH	55557	HT	55572	NH	55587	NH
55543	NH	55558	NH	55573	NH	55588	NH
55544	NH	55559	HT	55574	NH	55589	NH
55545	NH	55560	HT	55575	NH	55590	NH
55546	NH	55561	HT	55576	NH	55591	NH
55547	NH	55562	HT	55577	NH		
55548	NH	55563	HT	55578	NH		
55549	NH	55564	HA	55579	NH		
55550	NH	55565	NH	55580	NH		
55551	NH	55566	HT	55581	NH		
55552	NH	55567	NH	55582	NH		
55553	NH	55568	NH	55583	NH		
55554	NH	55569	NH	55584	NH		
55555	NH	55570	NH	55585	NH		
55556	NH	55571	NH	55586	NH		

Class 142 DMSL Leyland/BREL Railbus (142001-142050)

55592	NH	55605	NH	55618	NH	55631	NH
55593	NH	55606	NH	55619	NH	55632	NH
55594	NH	55607	HT	55620	NH	55633	NH
55595	NH	55608	NH	55621	NH	55634	NH
55596	NH	55609	HT	55622	NH	55635	NH
55597	NH	55610	HT	55623	NH	55636	NH
55598	NH	55611	HT	55624	NH	55637	NH
55599	NH	55612	HT	55625	NH	55638	NH
55600	NH	55613	HT	55626	NH	55639	NH
55601	NH	55614	HA	55627	NH	55640	NH
55602	NH	55615	NH	55628	NH	55641	NH
55603	NH	55616	HT	55629	NH		
55604	NH	55617	NH	55630	NH		

Class 143 DMS Alexander/Barclay Railbus (143001-143025)

55642	HT	55650	HT	55658	HT	55663	HT
55643	HT	55651	HT	55659	HT	55664	HT
55644	HT	55652	HT	55660	HT	55665	HT
55645	HT	55653	HT	55661	HT	55666	HT
55646	HT	55654	HT	55662	HT		
55647	HT	55655	HT				
55648	HT	55656	HT				
55649	HT	55657	HT				

Class 143 DMSL Alexander/Barclay Railbus (143001-143025)

55667	HT	55674	HT	55681	HT	55688	HT
55668	HT	55675	HT	55682	HT	55689	HT
55669	HT	55676	HT	55683	HT	55690	HT
55670	HT	55677	HT	55684	HT	55691	HT
55671	HT	55678	HT	55685	HT		
55672	HT	55679	HT	55686	HT		
55673	HT	55680	HT	55687	HT		

Class 142 DMS Leyland/BREL Railbus (142051-142096)

55701	NH	55705	NH	55709	NH	55713	NH
55702	NH	55706	NH	55710	NH	55714	NH
55703	NH	55707	NH	55711	NH	55715	NH
55704	NH	55708	NH	55712	NH	55716	NH

55717	NH	55725	NL	55733	NL	55741	NL
55718	NH	55726	NL	55734	NL	55742	NL
55719	NH	55727	NL	55735	NL	55743	NL
55720	NL	55728	NL	55736	NL	55744	NL
55721	NL	55729	NL	55737	NL	55745	NL
55722	NL	55730	NL	55738	NL	55746	NL
55723	NL	55731	NL	55739	NL		
55724	NL	55732	NL	55740	NL		

Class 142 DMSL Leyland/BREL Railbus (142051-142096)

55747	NH	55759	NH	55771	NL	55783	NL
55748	NH	55760	NH	55772	NL	55784	NL
55749	NH	55761	NH	55773	NL	55785	NL
55750	NH	55762	NH	55774	NL	55786	NL
55751	NH	55763	NH	55775	NL	55787	NL
55752	NH	55764	NH	55776	NL	55788	NL
55753	NH	55765	NH	55777	NL	55789	NL
55754	NH	55766	NL	55778	NL	55790	NL
55755	NH	55767	NL	55779	NL	55791	NL
55756	NH	55768	NL	55780	NL	55792	NL
55757	NH	55769	NL	55781	NL		
55758	NH	55770	NL	55782	NL		

Class 144 DMS Alexander/BREL Railbus (144001-144023)

55801	NL	55807	NL	55813	NL	55819	NL
55802	NL	55808	NL	55814	NL	55820	NL
55803	NL	55809	NL	55815	NL	55821	NL
55804	NL	55810	NL	55816	NL	55822	NL
55805	NL	55811	NL	55817	NL	55823	NL
55806	NL	55812	NL	55818	NL		

Class 144 DMSL Alexander/Barclay Railbus (144001-144023)

55824	NL	55830	NL	55837	NL	55844	NL
55825	NL	55831	NL	55838	NL	55845	NL
55825	NL	55832	NL	55839	NL	55846	NL
55826	NL	55833	NL	55840	NL		
55827	NL	55834	NL	55841	NL		
55828	NL	55835	NL	55842	NL		
55829	NL	55836	NL	55843	NL		

Class 144 MS Alexander/BREL Railbus (144014-144023)

55850	NL	55853	NL	55856	NL	55859	NL
55851	NL	55854	NL	55857	NL		
55852	NL	55855	NL	55858	NL		

Class 114 DMPMV Derby "Heavyweight" Parcels

55930	CA
55931	CA
55932	CA

Class 127 DMPMV Derby Suburban (Converted 1985 from DMBS)

55966	LO	55972	LO	55978	LO	55983	LO
55967	LO	55973	LO	55979	LO	55984	LO
55968	LO	55975	LO	55980	LO	55985	LO
55969	LO	55976	LO	55981	LO	55986	LO
55970	LO	55977	LO	55982	LO	55987	LO
55971	LO						

Class 128 DMPMV Gloucester RC&W

55991	CA	55994	CA
55992	CA	55995	CA
55993	CA		

Class 150/1 DMS BREL Sprinter (150101-150150)

57101	DY	57115	DY	57129	DY	57143	DY
57102	DY	57116	DY	57130	DY	57144	DY
57103	DY	57117	DY	57131	DY	57145	DY
57104	DY	57118	DY	57132	DY	57146	DY
57105	DY	57119	DY	57133	DY	57147	DY
57106	DY	57120	DY	57134	DY	57148	DY
57107	DY	57121	DY	57135	DY	57149	DY
57108	DY	57122	DY	57136	DY	57150	DY
57109	DY	57123	DY	57137	DY		
57110	DY	57124	DY	57138	DY		
57111	DY	57125	DY	57139	DY		
57112	DY	57126	DY	57140	DY		
57113	DY	57127	DY	57141	DY		
57114	DY	57128	DY	57142	DY		

Class 150/2 DMS BREL Sprinter (150201-150285)

57201	NH	57223	NH	57245	HA	57267	CF
57202	NL	57224	NL	57246	NL	57268	CF
57203	NH	57225	NH	57247	CF	57269	CF
57204	NL	57226	NL	57248	NL	57270	CF
57205	DY	57227	NH	57249	CF	57271	CF
57206	NL	57228	NL	57250	NL	57272	CF
57207	NH	57229	NH	57251	CF	57273	CF
57208	HA	57230	NL	57252	NL	57274	CF
57209	NH	57231	NH	57253	DY	57275	CF
57210	NL	57232	NL	57254	NL	57276	CF
57211	NH	57233	NH	57255	HA	57277	CF
57212	DY	57234	NL	57256	NL	57278	CF
57213	NH	57235	NH	57257	HA	57279	CF
57214	NL	57236	NL	57258	NL	57280	CF
57215	NH	57237	NH	57259	HA	57281	CF
57216	NL	57238	NL	57260	NL	57282	CF
57217	NH	57239	NH	57261	CF	57283	HA
57218	NL	57240	NL	57262	NL	57284	HA
57219	NH	57241	NH	57263	CF	57285	HA
57220	NL	57242	NL	57264	HA		
57221	NH	57243	NH	57265	CF		
57222	NL	57244	NL	57266	CF		

Class 155 DMS Leyland Super Sprinter (155301-155347)

57301	CF	57312	CF	57323	CF	57334	CF
57302	CF	57313	CF	57324	CF	57335	CF
57303	CF	57314	CF	57325	CF	57341	NL
57304	CF	57315	CF	57326	CF	57342	NL
57305	CF	57316	CF	57327	CF	57343	NL
57306	CF	57317	CF	57328	CF	57344	NL
57307	CF	57318	CF	57329	CF	57345	NL
57308	CF	57319	CF	57330	CF	57346	NL
57309	CF	57320	CF	57331	CF	57347	NL
57310	CF	57321	CF	57332	CF		
57311	CF	57322	CF	57333	CF		

Class 156 DMS Metro-Cammell Super Sprinter (156401-156514)

57401	NC	57403	NC	57405	NC	57407	NC
57402	NC	57404	NC	57406	NC	57408	NC

57409 NC
57410 NC
57411 NC
57412 NC
57413 NC
57414 NC
57415 NC
57416 NC
57417 NC
57418 NC
57419 NC
57420 NC
57421 NC
57422 NC
57423 NC
57424 NC
57425 NC
57426 NC
57427 NC
57428 NC
57429 NC
57430 CK
57431 CK
57432 CK
57433 CK
57434 CK
57435 CK
57436 CK
57437 CK
57438 NC
57439 CK
57440 NC
57441 NL
57442 CK
57443 NL
57444 NL
57445 IS
57446 IS
57447 IS
57448 IS
57449 IS
57450 IS
57451 IS
57452 IS
57453 IS
57454 IS
57455 IS
57456 HA
57457 HA
57458 HA
57459 HA
57460 HA
57461 HA
57462
57463
57464
57465
57466
57467
57468
57469
57470
57471
57472
57473
57474
57475
57476
57477
57478
57479
57480
57481
57482
57483
57484
57485
57486
57487
57488
57489
57490
57491
57492
57493
57494
57495
57496
57497
57498
57499
57500
57501
57502
57503
57504
57505
57506
57507
57508
57509
57510
57511
57512
57513
57514

Class 158 DMS Super Sprinter (158701-158808)

57701
57702
57703
57704
57705
57706
57707
57708
57709
57710
57711
57712
57713
57714
57715
57716
57717
57718
57719
57720
57721
57722
57723
57724
57725
57726
57727
57728
57729
57730
57731
57732
57733
57734
57735
57736
57737
57738
57739
57740
57741
57742
57743
57744
57745
57746
57747
57748
57749
57750
57751
57752

57753	57765	57777	57789
57754	57766	57778	57790
57755	57767	57779	57791
57756	57768	57780	57792
57757	57769	57781	57793
57758	57770	57782	57794
57759	57771	57783	57795
57760	57772	57784	57796
57761	57773	57785	57797
57762	57774	57786	
57763	57775	57787	
57764	57776	57788	

Class 158 MS Super Sprinter

58701	58705	58709	58713
58702	58706	58710	
58703	58707	58711	
58704	58708	58712	

Class 116 TS Derby "Suburban"

59032	TS
59040	HTu

Class 101 TSL Metro-Cammell

59042	HA

Class 101 TBSL Metro-Cammell

59049	ED
59050	LE
59055	NC

Class 101 TSL Metro-Cammell

59061	HA
59065	HA
59072	HA

Class 101 TBSL Metro-Cammell

59073	HA	59080	HA
59074	ED	59082	ED
59077	NC	59084	NC
59079	NC	59085	NC

Class 101 TSL Metro-Cammell

59086	HA
59090	ED
59091	RG

Class 101 TBSL Metro-Cammell

59092	NC
59093	NL
59095	NC

Class 101 TSL Metro-Cammell

59101	RG
59104	HA
59105	RG
59107	HA

Class 101 TBSL Metro-Cammell

59113	NL

Class 101 TCL Metro-Cammell

59115	RG	59117	RG	59124	HA	59128	RG
59116	HA	59118	LA	59125	RG	59130	LA

Class 104 TCL Birmingham RC&W

59137	BX	59149	BX	59155	BX	59183	BX
59144	BX	59152	BX	59163	BY	59187	BX
59148	BX	59153	HA	59168	NL		

Class 104 TSL Birmingham RC&W

59195	NH
59206	BY
59207	BX

Class 108 TBSL Derby "Lightweight"

59245	HA
59246	NL
59248	HA
59249	NL
59250	NL

Class 101 TS Metro-Cammell

59302	HA
59303	HA
59304	HA
59305	HA
59306	RG

Class 116 TC Derby "Suburban"

59330	TSu
59335	TS
59344	TS
59353	TS
59367	TS

Class 108 TSL Derby "Lightweight"

59380	LE	59383	LE	59386	HA	59389	BX
59381	LE	59384	LE	59387	HA	59390	BX
59382	LE	59385	LE	59388	BX		

Class 119 TSLRB Gloucester "Cross-Country"

59416	RG	59430	RG
59419	RG	59435	RG
59421	RG	59437	RG
59424	RG		
59425	RG		

Class 116 TC Derby "Suburban"

59442	TS
59444	TS
59445	TS
59446	TS
59448	TS

Class 118 TCL Birmingham RC&W "Suburban"

59473	TS
59478	TS
59481	TS
59482	LA
59483	TS

Class 117 TCL Pressed Steel "Suburban"

59484	RG	59494	RG	59504	TS	59514	RG
59485	RG	59495	RG	59505	TS	59515	RG
59486	TS	59496	RG	59506	RG	59516	TS
59487	RG	59497	RG	59507	RG	59517	TS
59488	RG	59498	RG	59508	RG	59518	RG
59489	RG	59499	RG	59509	TS	59519	RG
59490	TS	59500	TS	59510	RG	59520	TS
59491	RG	59501	RG	59511	RG	59521	TS
59492	TS	59502	RG	59512	TS	59522	TS
59493	RG	59503	RG	59513	RG		

Class 101 TCL Metro-Cammell

59525	HA	59536	NC	59543	RG	59565	NL
59526	RG	59539	CF	59553	HA		
59530	RG	59540	RG	59561	LA		
59532	HA	59542	ED	59562	NL		

Class 101 TSL Metro-Cammell

59570	RG
59571	HA

Class 127 TSL Derby "Suburban"

59589	TS	59596	TS	59606	TS	59613	TS
59590	TS	59597	TS	59607	TS	59614	TS
59591	TS	59598	TS	59608	TS	59615	TS
59592	TS	59600	TS	59609	TS	59616	TS
59593	TS	59602	TS	59610	TS	59617	TS
59594	TS	59603	TS	59611	TS		
59595	TS	59604	TS	59612	TS		

Class 127 TS Derby "Suburban"

59621	TSu	59627	TSu	59632	TS	59648	TS
59622	TSu	59629	TS	59641	TS		
59625	TS	59631	TSu	59643	TS		

Class 115 TS Derby "Suburban"

59651	BY	59655	BY	59659	BY	59663	BY
59652	BY	59656	BY	59660	BY		
59653	TSu	59657	BY	59661	TS		
59654	BY	59658	TS	59662	BY		

Class 115 TCL Derby "Suburban"

59664	BY	59669	BY	59674	TS
59665	BY	59670	TS	59675	BY
59666	TSu	59671	BY	59676	BY
59667	BY	59672	TS	59677	TS
59668	TS	59673	TS	59678	BY

Class 101 TCL Metro-Cammell

59688	HA
59690	NL

Class 110 TSL Birmingham RC&W "Calder Valley"

59694	NL	59709	LE
59696	HA	59710	HA
59697	HA		
59701	HA		

Class 115 TS Derby "Suburban"

59713	TS
59715	TSu
59716	TSu
59717	TSu

Class 115 TCL Derby "Suburban"

59719	TS	59722	TS
59720	TS	59723	TS
59721	TS	59724	TS

Class 115 TS Derby "Suburban"

59725	TSu	59731	BY	59736	BY	59741	TS
59726	TS	59732	BY	59737	BY	59743	TS
59727	BY	59733	BY	59738	BY	59744	TSu
59728	BY	59734	BY	59739	BY		
59729	BY	59735	BY	59740	BY		

Class 115 TCL Derby "Suburban"

59745	TS	59750	BY	59755	BY	59760	TS
59746	BY	59751	TS	59756	TS	59761	BY
59747	BY	59752	BY	59757	TS	59762	BY
59748	NHu	59753	TS	59758	BY	59763	BY
59749	BY	59754	BY	59759	BY	59764	BY

Class 107 TSL Derby "Heavyweight"

59782	ED	59790	ED	59796	ED	59803	ED
59783	ED	59791	HA	59797	HA	59804	ED
59784	ED	59792	ED	59798	ED	59805	ED
59785	HA	59793	ED	59800	HA	59806	ED
59786	HA	59794	HA	59801	ED	59807	ED
59789	HA	59795	ED	59802	ED		

Class 110 TSL Birmingham RC&W "Calder Valley"

59809	HA	59812	NHu
59810	HA	59817	HA

Class 111 DHCL Metro-Cammell/Rolls Royce

78709	NL	78713	NL	78718	NL
78711	NL	78714	NL	78719	NL
78712	NL	78717	NL	78722	NL

Class 111 DHBS Metro-Cammell/Rolls Royce

78959	NL	78962	NL	78968	NL
78960	NL	78964	NL	78969	NL
78961	NL	78967	NL	78971	NL

DIESEL ELECTRIC MULTIPLE UNITS

Class 203 4L

203001 SU (vehicle 60014 named St.Leonards)

Class 205 3H

205001	SU	205015	SU	205025	EH	205030	EH
205002	SU	205016	SU	205026	EH	205031	EH
205008	SU	205018	SU	205027	EH	205032	EH
205009	SU	205023	SU	205028	EH	205033	EH
205012	SU	205024	SU	205029	EH		

Class 205/1 3H

205101 SU

Class 207 3D

207001	SU	207010	EH
207002	SU	207011	SU
207004	SU	207013	EH
207005	EH	207017	EH
207008	SU	207019	SU

ELECTRIC MULTIPLE UNITS

Class 487 Waterloo & City (Motor 51-62 Trailer 71-86)

51	WC	59	WC	74	WC	81	WC
53	WC	60	WC	75	WC	83	WC
54	WC	61	WC	76	WC	84	WC
55	WCu	62	WC	77	WC	85	WC
56	WC	71	WCu	78	WC	86	WC
57	WC	72	WC	79	WCu		
58	WC	73	WC	80	WC		

Set Nos

Class 421/1 4-CIG

1100	BI	1111	BI	1118	BI
1105	BI	1114	BI	1123	BI
1110	BI	1116	BI	1127	BI

Class 421/2 4-CIG

1201	BI	1223	FR	1261	FR	1286	BI
1202	BI	1224	FR	1262	BI	1287	BI
1203	BI	1225	FR	1263	BI	1288	BI
1204	BI	1226	FR	1264	BI	1289	BI
1205	BI	1238	FR	1266	BI	1290	BI
1206	BI	1241	FR	1268	BI	1291	BI
1208	FR	1243	FR	1269	BI	1292	BI
1209	FR	1244	FR	1270	BI	1293	BI
1210	FR	1245	FR	1271	BI	1294	BI
1211	FR	1246	FR	1272	BI	1295	BI
1212	FR	1247	FR	1274	BI	1296	BI
1213	FR	1249	FR	1275	BI	1297	BI
1214	FR	1252	FR	1276	BI	1298	BI
1215	FR	1253	FR	1277	BI	1299	BI
1216	FR	1254	FR	1278	BI	1300	BI
1217	FR	1255	FR	1279	BI		
1218	FR	1256	BI	1280	BI		
1219	FR	1257	BI	1281	BI		
1220	FR	1258	FR	1282	BI		
1221	FR	1259	FR	1284	BI		
1222	FR	1260	FR	1285	BI		

Class 411 Refurbished 4-CEP

1500	RE	1531	RE	1562	RE	1593	RE
1501	RE	1532	RE	1563	RE	1594	RE
1502	RE	1533	RE	1564	RE	1595	RE
1503	RE	1534	RE	1565	RE	1596	RE
1504	RE	1535	RE	1566	RE	1597	RE
1505	RE	1536	RE	1567	RE	1598	RE
1506	RE	1537	RE	1568	RE	1599	RE
1507	RE	1538	RE	1569	RE	1600	RE
1508	RE	1539	RE	1570	RE	1601	RE
1509	RE	1540	RE	1571	RE	1602	RE
1510	RE	1541	RE	1572	RE	1603	RE
1511	RE	1542	RE	1573	RE	1604	RE
1512	RE	1543	RE	1574	RE	1605	RE
1513	RE	1544	RE	1575	RE	1606	RE
1514	RE	1545	RE	1576	RE	1607	RE
1515	RE	1546	RE	1577	RE	1608	RE
1516	RE	1547	RE	1578	RE	1609	RE
1517	RE	1548	RE	1579	RE	1610	RE
1518	RE	1549	RE	1580	RE	1611	RE
1519	RE	1550	RE	1581	RE	1612	RE
1520	RE	1551	RE	1582	RE	1613	RE
1521	RE	1552	RE	1583	RE	1614	RE
1522	RE	1553	RE	1584	RE	1615	RE
1523	RE	1554	RE	1585	RE	1616	RE
1524	RE	1555	RE	1586	RE	1617	RE
1525	RE	1556	RE	1587	RE	1618	RE
1526	RE	1557	RE	1588	RE	1619	RE
1527	RE	1558	RE	1589	RE	1620	RE
1528	RE	1559	RE	1590	RE	1621	RE
1529	RE	1560	RE	1591	RE		
1530	RE	1561	RE	1592	RE		

Class 421/3 Facelifted 4-CIG

1701	BI	1708	BI	1715	BI	1722	BI
1702	BI	1709	BI	1716	BI	1723	BI
1703	BI	1710	BI	1717	BI	1724	BI
1704	BI	1711	BI	1718	BI	1725	BI
1705	BI	1712	BI	1719	BI	1726	BI
1706	BI	1713	BI	1720	BI	1727	BI
1707	BI	1714	BI	1721	BI	1728	BI

1729	BI	1732	BI	1735		1738	
1730	BI	1733		1736		1739	
1731	BI	1734		1737		1740	

Class 421/4 Facelifted 4-CIG

1801	BI	1826		1851		1876	
1802	BI	1827		1852		1877	
1803	BI	1828		1853		1878	
1804	BI	1829		1854		1879	
1805	BI	1830		1855		1880	
1806	BI	1831		1856		1881	
1807	BI	1832		1857		1882	
1808	BI	1833		1858		1883	
1809	BI	1834		1859		1884	
1810	BI	1835		1860		1885	
1811	BI	1836		1861		1886	
1812	BI	1837		1862		1887	
1813	BI	1838		1863		1888	
1814	FR	1839		1864		1889	
1815	FR	1840		1865		1890	
1816	FR	1841		1866		1891	
1817	FR	1842		1867		1892	
1818	FR	1843		1868		1893	
1819	FR	1844		1869		1894	
1820	BI	1845		1870		1895	
1821	BI	1846		1871		1896	
1822	BI	1847		1872		1897	
1823	BI	1848		1873		1898	
1824	FR	1849		1874		1899	
1825	BI	1850		1875		1900	

Class 431 4-REP

1901(2001) BM
1902(   )
1903(   )

Class 432 4-REP

2003 BM
2007 BM

Class 422/1 4-BIG

2101	BI	2105	BI	2109	BI
2102	BI	2106	BI	2110	BI
2103	BI	2107	BI	2111	BI
2104	BI	2108	BI		

Class 422/2 4-BIG (to be renumbered in 18xx series)

2203	BI	2208	BI
2204	BI	2209	BI
2205	BI	2210	BI
2206	BI		

Class 412 Refurbished 4-BEP

2301	FR	2305	FR
2302	FR	2306	FR
2303	FR	2307	FR
2304	FR		

Class 442 (Bournemouth Express)

2401	BM	2407	BM	2413	BM	2419	BM
2402	BM	2408	BM	2414	BM	2420	BM
2403	BM	2409	BM	2415	BM	2421	BM
2404	BM	2410	BM	2416	BM	2422	BM
2405	BM	2411	BM	2417	BM	2423	BM
2406	BM	2412	BM	2418	BM	2424	BM

Class 492/8 4-TCB

2804	BM
2807	BM

Class 423 4-VEP

3000	BI	3004	BM	3008	BM	3012	BM
3001	BM	3005	BM	3009	BM	3013	BM
3002	BM	3006	BM	3010	BM	3014	BM
3003	BM	3007	BM	3011	BM	3015	BM

3016	BM	3087	BI	3126	WD	3160	RE
3017	BM	3088	BI	3127	WD	3161	RE
3018	BM	3089	BI	3128	WD	3162	RE
3019	BM	3090	BI	3129	WD	3163	RE
3020	BM	3091	BI	3130	WD	3164	RE
3026	BI	3092	BI	3131	WD	3165	RE
3030	BM	3093	BI	3132	WD	3166	RE
3032	BM	3094	BI	3133	WD	3167	RE
3033	BM	3095	BI	3134	BI	3169	RE
3034	BM	3096	BI	3135	BI	3170	RE
3035	BM	3097	BI	3136	BI	3171	RE
3037	BM	3098	BI	3137	BI	3172	RE
3046	FR	3099	BI	3138	RE	3173	RE
3053	FR	3103	BI	3139	BI	3174	RE
3056	FR	3106	BI	3140	BI	3175	RE
3058	FR	3107	BI	3141	WD	3176	RE
3059	FR	3108	BI	3142	WD	3177	RE
3067	WD	3109	BI	3143	WD	3178	RE
3068	FR	3110	BI	3144	WD	3179	RE
3069	FR	3111	BI	3145	FR	3180	RE
3070	WD	3112	BI	3146	FR	3181	RE
3071	WD	3113	WD	3147	FR	3182	RE
3072	WD	3114	WD	3148	RE	3183	RE
3073	WD	3115	WD	3149	RE	3184	RE
3074	WD	3116	WD	3150	RE	3185	RE
3075	WD	3117	WD	3151	RE	3186	RE
3076	WD	3118	WD	3152	RE	3187	RE
3077	WD	3119	WD	3153	RE	3188	RE
3078	WD	3120	WD	3154	RE	3189	RE
3080	BI	3121	WD	3155	RE	3190	RE
3083	BI	3122	WD	3156	RE	3191	RE
3084	BI	3123	WD	3157	RE	3192	RE
3085	BI	3124	WD	3158	RE	3193	RE
3086	BI	3125	WD	3159	RE	3194	RE

Class 413/2 4-CAP

3201	RE	3207	RE	3211	RE
3202	RE	3208	RE	3212	RE
3203	RE	3209	RE	3213	RE
3204	RE	3210	RE		
3205	RE				
3206	RE				

Class 413/3 4-CAP

3301	RE	3305	RE	3309	RE
3302	RE	3306	RE	3310	RE
3303	RE	3307	RE	3311	RE
3304	RE	3308	RE		

Class 423/
1 4-VEP

3421(3168)RE	3435(3025)BI	3449(3022)RE	3463( )
3422(3040)RE	3436(3029)BI	3450(3065)RE	3464( )
3423(3061)RE	3437(3027)BI	3451(3079)RE	3465( )
3424(3031)RE	3438(3100)BI	3452(3024)RE	3466( )
3425(3023)BM	3439(3055)BI	3453(3045)RE	3467( )
3426(3047)BM	3440(3102)BI	3454(3049)RE	3468( )
3427(3041)BM	3441(3043)BI	3455(3048)FR	3469( )
3428(3062)BM	3442(3081)BI	3456(3063)FR	3470( )
3429(3021)BM	3443(3082)BI	3457(3050)FR	3471( )
3430(3028)WD	3444(3038)BI	3458(3051)FR	3472( )
3431(3064)WD	3445(3060)RE	3459(3052)FR	3473( )
3432(3054)WD	3446(3101)RE	3460(3105)BI	3474( )
3433(3057)WD	3447(3044)RE	3461(3104)BI	3475( )
3434(3066)WD	3448(3042)RE	3462( )	

Class 414 2-HAP

4201	WD	4306	WD	4312	WD	4318	WD
4301	WD	4307	WD	4313	WD	4319	WD
4302	WD	4308	WD	4314	WD	4320	WD
4303	WD	4309	WD	4315	WD	4321	WD
4304	WD	4310	WD	4316	WD	4322	WD
4305	WD	4311	WD	4317	WD		

Class 405 4-SUB

4732 SU

Note: This unit is painted green and is kept for special workings.

Class 415/1 4-EPB

5104	SG	5107	SG	5113	SG	5114	SG

5115	SG	5159	SG	5196	SG	5243	SG
5121	SG	5160	SG	5201	SG	5248	SG
5124	SG	5163	SG	5202	SG	5261	SG
5126	SG	5166	SG	5209	SG	5264	SG
5131	SG	5168	SG	5210	SG	5265(5001)	SG
5133	SG	5169	SG	5213	SG	5266(5020)	SG
5134	SG	5170	SG	5217	SG	5267(5027)	SG
5138	SG	5173	SG	5220	SG	5268(5035)	SG
5139	SG	5174	SG	5222	SG	5269(5039)	SG
5145	SG	5176	SG	5223	SG	5270(5040)	SG
5146	SG	5177	SG	5226	SG	5271(5042)	SG
5148	SG	5182	SG	5228	SG	5272(5044)	SG
5150	SG	5185	SG	5229	SG	5273(5045)	SG
5153	SG	5189	SG	5230	SG	5274(5046)	SG
5154	SG	5190	SG	5231	SG	5275(5049)	SG
5155	SG	5191	SG	5232	SG	5276(5051)	SG
5156	SG	5194	SG	5240	SG	5277(5052)	SG
5157	SG	5195	SG	5242	SG		

Class 415/4 Facelifted 4-EPB

5401	SU	5423	SU	5445	SU	5467	SG
5402	SU	5424	SU	5446	SU	5468	SG
5403	SU	5425	SU	5447	SU	5469	SG
5404	SU	5426	SU	5448	SU	5470	SG
5405	SU	5427	SU	5449	SU	5471	SG
5406	SU	5428	SU	5450	SU	5472	SG
5407	SU	5429	SU	5451	SU	5473	SG
5408	SU	5430	SU	5452	SG	5474	SG
5409	SU	5431	SU	5453	SG	5475	SG
5410	SU	5432	SU	5454	SG	5476	SG
5411	SU	5433	SU	5455	SG	5477	SG
5412	SU	5434	SU	5456	SG	5478	SG
5413	SU	5435	SU	5457	SG	5479	SG
5414	SU	5436	SU	5458	SG	5480	SG
5415	SU	5437	SU	5459	SG	5481	SG
5416	SU	5438	SU	5460	SG	5482	SG
5417	SU	5439	SU	5461	SG	5483	SG
5418	SU	5440	SU	5462	SG	5484	SG
5419	SU	5441	SU	5463	SG	5485	SG
5420	SU	5442	SU	5464	SG	5486	SG
5421	SU	5443	SU	5465	SG	5487	SG
5422	SU	5444	SU	5466	SG	5488	SG

5489 SG
5490 SG
5491 SG
5492 SG
5493 SG
5494 SG
5495 SG
5496 SG
5497 SG

Class 415/5 4-EPB

5501(5125) SG
5502(5183) SG
5503(5140) SG
5504(5038) SG
5505(5162) SG
5506(5151) SG
5507(5171) SG
5508(5018) SG
5509(5119) SG
5510(5172) SG
5511(5016) SG
5512(5105) SG
5513(5179) SG
5514(5184) SG
5515(5207) SG
5516(5032) SG
5517(5022) SG
5518(5147) SG
5519(5137) SG
5520(5111) SG
5521(5135) SG
5522(5197) SG
5523(5116) SG
5524(5144) SG
5525(5136) SG
5526(5187) SG
5527(5117) SG
5528(5129) SG
5529(5043) SG
5530(5101) SG
5531(5005) SG
5532(5013) SG

Class 415/6 4-EPB

5601 SG
5602 SG
5603 SG
5604 SG
5605 SG
5606 SG
5610 SG
5611 SG
5612 SG
5613 SG
5614 SG
5615 SG
5616 SG
5617 SG
5618 SG
5619 SG
5620 SG
5621 SG
5622 SG
5623 SG
5624 SG
5625 SG

Class 415/7 4-EPB

5626(5607) SG
5627(5608) SG
5628(5609) SG

Class 455/7

5701 WD
5702 WD
5703 WD
5704 WD
5705 WD
5706 WD
5707 WD
5708 WD
5709 WD
5710 WD
5711 WD
5712 WD
5713 WD
5714 WD
5715 WD
5716 WD
5717 WD
5718 WD
5719 WD
5720 WD
5721 WD
5722 WD
5723 WD
5724 WD
5725 WD
5726 WD
5727 WD
5728 WD
5729 WD
5730 WD
5731 WD
5732 WD
5733 WD
5734 WD
5735 WD
5736 WD
5737 WD
5738 WD
5739 WD
5740 WD
5741 WD
5742 WD
5743 WD

Class 455/8

5801	SU	5820	SU	5839	WD	5858	WD
5802	SU	5821	SU	5840	WD	5859	WD
5803	SU	5822	SU	5841	WD	5860	WD
5804	SU	5823	SU	5842	WD	5861	WD
5805	SU	5824	SU	5843	WD	5862	WD
5806	SU	5825	SU	5844	WD	5863	WD
5807	SU	5826	SU	5845	WD	5864	WD
5808	SU	5827	SU	5846	WD	5865	WD
5809	SU	5828	SU	5847	WD	5866	WD
5810	SU	5829	SU	5848	WD	5867	WD
5811	SU	5830	SU	5849	WD	5868	WD
5812	SU	5831	SU	5850	WD	5869	WD
5813	SU	5832	SU	5851	WD	5870	WD
5814	SU	5833	SU	5852	WD	5871	WD
5815	SU	5834	SU	5853	WD	5872	WD
5816	SU	5835	SU	5854	WD	5873	WD
5817	SU	5836	WD	5855	WD	5874	WD
5818	SU	5837	WD	5856	WD		
5819	SU	5838	WD	5857	WD		

Class 455/9

5901	WD	5906	WD	5911	WD	5916	WD
5902	WD	5907	WD	5912	WD	5917	WD
5903	WD	5908	WD	5913	WD	5918	WD
5904	WD	5909	WD	5914	WD	5919	WD
5905	WD	5910	WD	5915	WD	5920	WD

Class 416/2 2-EPB

6202	SG	6223	SG	6237	SG	6251	SG
6203	SG	6224	SG	6238	SG	6253	SG
6205	SG	6225	SG	6239	SG	6255	SG
6207	SG	6226	SG	6240	SG	6256	SG
6212	SG	6227	SG	6241	SG	6257	SG
6213	SG	6229	SG	6243	SG	6259	SG
6217	SG	6230	SG	6244	SG	6260	SG
6218	SG	6231	SG	6245	SG	6261	SG
6221	SG	6235	SG	6247	SG	6262	SG
6222	SG	6236	SG	6249	SG	6263	SG

6264	SG	6269	SG	6273	SG	6277	SG
6265	SG	6270	SG	6274	SG	6278	SG
6267	SG	6271	SG	6275	SG		
6268	SG	6272	SG	6276	SG		

Class 416/3 2-EPB

6301	SU	6311	SU	6322	SU	6332	SU
6302	SU	6312	SU	6323	SU	6333	SU
6303	SU	6314	SU	6324	SU	6334	SU
6304	SU	6315	SU	6325	SU	6335(6313)	SU
6305	SU	6316	SU	6326	SU		
6306	SU	6317	SU	6327	SU		
6307	SU	6318	SU	6328	SU		
6308	SU	6319	SU	6329	SU		
6309	SU	6320	SU	6330	SU		
6310	SU	6321	SU	6331	SU		

Class 416/4 Facelifted 2-EPB

6401	SG	6406	SG	6411	SG	6416	SG
6402	SG	6407	SG	6412	SG	6417	SG
6403	SG	6408	SG	6413	SG	6418	SG
6404	SG	6409	SG	6414	SG		
6405	SG	6410	SG	6415	SG		

Class 457(Prototype)

7001 SH

Class 438 4-TC

8001	BM	8010	BM	8017	BM	8026	BM
8004(2808)	BM	8012	BM	8018	BM	8027	BM
8006	BM	8014	BM	8021	BM		
8007	BM	8015	BM	8023	BM		

Class 488 Victoria-Gatwick Sets

488/2

8201	SL	72500/72638	8202	SL	72501/72639

8203	SL	72502/72640	8207	SL	72506/72642
8204	SL	72503/72641	8208	SL	72507/72643
8205	SL	72504/72628	8209	SL	72508/72644
8206	SL	72505/72629	8210	SL	72509/72635

488/3

8302	SL	72602/72701/72604
8303	SL	72603/72702/72608
8304	SL	72606/72703/72611
8305	SL	72605/72704/72609
8306	SL	72607/72705/72610
8307	SL	72612/72706/72613
8308	SL	72614/72707/72615
8309	SL	72616/72708/72617
8310	SL	72618/72709/72619
8311	SL	72620/72710/72621
8312	SL	72622/72711/72623
8313	SL	72624/72712/72625
8314	SL	72626/72713/72627
8315	SL	72636/72714/72645
8316	SL	72630/72715/72631
8317	SL	72632/72716/72633
8318	SL	72634/72717/72637
8319	SL	72646/72718/72647

Class 419 MLV

9001	RE	9006	RE
9002	RE	9007	RE
9003	RE	9008	RE
9004	RE	9009	RE
9005	RE	9010	RE

Class 489 GLV Victoria-Gatwick

9101	SL	9107	SL
9102	SL	9108	SL
9103	SL	9109	SL
9104	SL	9110	SL
9105	SL		
9106	SL		

Class 504 **Car Nos**

65444	BQ	65455	BQ	77168	BQ	77179	BQ
65445	BQ	65456	BQ	77170	BQ	77180	BQ
65446	BQ	65457	BQ	77171	BQ	77181	BQ
65447	BQ	65458	BQ	77172	BQ	77182	BQ
65449	BQ	65459	BQ	77173	BQ		
65450	BQ	65460	BQ	77174	BQ		
65451	BQ	65461	BQ	77175	BQ		
65452	BQ	77165	BQ	77176	BQ		
65453	BQ	77166	BQ	77177	BQ		
65454	BQ	77167	BQ	77178	BQ		

Class 485 5-VEC **Set Nos**

485041	RY	1-27-92-26-2
485042	RY	3-29-95-47-4
485043	RY	5-31-43-32-6
485044	RY	7-33-44-49-8
485045	RY	9-93-94-34-10

Class 302

302200	EM	(302207)	302220	EM	
302201	EM		302221	EM	
302202	EM		302222	EM	
302203	EM	(302263)	302223	EM	(302293)
302204	EM		302224	EM	
302205	EM		302225	EM	
302206	EM		302226	EM	
302207	EM	(302310)	302227	EM	(302277)
302208	EM	(302308)	302228	EM	
302209	EM		302229	EM	
302210	EM		302230	EM	(302232)
302211	EM		302231	IL	
302212	EM		302234	IL	
302213	EM		302235	IL	
302214	EM	(302304)	302237	IL	
302215	EM		302238	IL	(302312)
302216	EM		302239	IL	
302217	EM		302241	IL	
302218	EM		302243	ILu	
302219	EM		302244	IL	

302245	IL	
302246	IL	
302247	ILu	
302248	EMu	
302249	EM	
302250	EM	(302300)
302251	EM	
302252	IL	
302253	EM	(302301)
302254	EM	
302255	EM	(302303)
302256	IL	
302257	IL	
302258	IL	
302259	IL	
302260	EM	(302302)
302262	EM	
302264	EM	
302265	IL	
302267	EM	(302307)
302268	IL	
302269	IL	
302270	EM	
302272	EM	
302273	EM	(302306)
302274	EM	
302275	EM	(302311)
302276	EM	(302208)
302278	EM	
302280	EM	
302282	EM	
302283	IL	
302284	EM	
302285	IL	
302286	EM	
302289	IL	
302290	IL	
302291	EMu	
302292	EM	
302295	ILu	
302296	EM	
302297	IL	
302298	EM	
302299	EM	

Class 303

303001	GW
303003	GW
303004	GW
303005	GW
303006	GW
303008	GW
303009	GW
303010	GW
303011	GW
303012	GW
303013	GW
303014	GW
303016	GW
303019	GW
303020	GW
303021	GW
303023	GW
303024	GW
303025	GW
303027	GW
303028	GW
303029	GW
303032	GW
303034	GW
303036	LG
303037	GW
303038	GW
303039	GW
303040	GW
303041	LG
303042	GW
303043	GW
303044	GW
303045	GW
303046	GW
303047	GW
303048	LG
303049	LG
303050	LG
303052	GW
303053	LG
303054	GW
303055	GW
303056	GW
303057	LG
303058	GW
303060	LG
303061	GW
303062	GW
303063	GW
303064	GW
303065	GW
303066	LG
303067	LG
303068	GW
303069	GW
303070	GW
303071	GW
303072	GW
303073	GW
303075	GW
303076	GW
303077	GW
303078	LG
303079	GW
303080	GW
303082	LG
303083	GW

303085	GW	303087	GW	303089	GW	303091	GW
303086	GW	303088	GW	303090	GW		

Class 304

304001	LG	304011	LG	304023	LG	304036	LG
304002	LG	304012	LG	304024	LG	304037	LG
304003	LG	304013	LG	304027	LG	304039	LG
304004	LG	304014	LG	304028	LG	304040	LG
304005	LG	304015	LG	304029	LG	304041	LG
304006	LG	304016	LG	304030	LG	304042	LG
304007	LG	304017	LG	304032	LG	304043	LG
304008	LG	304019	LG	304033	LG	304045	LG
304009	LG	304020	LG	304034	LG		
304010	LG	304021	LG	304035	LG		

Class 305/1

305401	IL	305407	IL	305413	IL	305419	IL
305402	IL	305408	IL	305414	IL	305420	IL
305403	IL	305409	IL	305415	IL	305421	IL
305404	IL	305410	IL	305416	IL	305422	IL
305405	IL	305411	IL	305417	IL		
305406	IL	305412	IL	305418	IL		

Class 305/2

305501	EM	305506	EM	305511	IL	305516	IL
305502	EM	305507	EM	305512	IL	305517	IL
305503	EM	305508	EM	305513	IL	305518	IL
305504	IL	305509	EM	305514	IL	305519	IL
305505	IL	305510	EM	305515	IL		

Class 305/3 *used as a mobile classroom

305521	EM	305524	EM	305527	EM
305522	EM	305525	EM	305528	EM
305523	EM	305526	EM	305935 *	ER

Class 306

306017 IL — Note: This unit is painted green and is used for special workings.

Class 307

307101	IL	307109	IL	307117	IL	307125	IL
307102	IL	307110	IL	307118	IL	307126	IL
307103	IL	307111	IL	307119	IL	307127	IL
307104	IL	307112	IL	307120	IL	307128	IL
307105	IL	307113	IL	307121	IL	307129	IL
307106	IL	307114	IL	307122	IL	307130	IL
307107	IL	307115	IL	307123	IL	307131	IL
307108	IL	307116	IL	307124	IL	307132	IL

Class 308/1

308133	IL	308142	EM	308151	EM	308160	EM
308134	IL	308143	EM	308152	EM	308161	EM
308135	IL	308144	EM	308153	EM	308162	EM
308136	IL	308145	EM	308154	EM	308163	EM
308137	IL	308146	EM	308155	EM	308164	EM
308138	IL	308147	EM	308156	EM	308165	EM
308139	IL	308148	IL	308157	EM		
308140	EM	308149	IL	308158	EM		
308141	EM	308150	IL	308159	EM		

Class 308/2 *in departmental use

308991 *	IL
308993	IL
308994	IL
308995	IL

Class 309/1 Essex Express Stock

309601	CC	309603	CC	309605	CC	309607	CC
309602	CC	309604	CC	309606	CC	309608	CC

Class 309/2 Essex Express Stock

309611	CC	309616	CC	309623	CC
309612	CC	309617	CC	309624	CC
309613	CC	309618	CC	309625	CC
309614	CC	309621	CC	309626	CC
309615	CC	309622	CC	309627	CC

Class 310

310046	EM	310059	EM	310072	EM	310087	EM
310047	EM	310060	IL	310074	EM	310088	EM
310048	BY	310061	EM	310075	EM	310089	EM
310049	EM	310062	BY	310077	EM	310091	EM
310050	EM	310063	BY	310079	EM	310092	EM
310051	BY	310064	EM	310080	EM	310093	EM
310052	EM	310065	EM	310081	EM	310094	IL
310053	BY	310066	EM	310082	EM	310095	EM
310054	BY	310067	EM	310083	EM		
310056	IL	310068	EM	310084	EM		
310057	EM	310069	EM	310085	EM		
310058	BY	310070	EM	310086	BY		

Class 310/1

310101	BY	(310073)	310106	( )
310102	BY	(310055)	310107	( )
310103	BY	(310076)	310108	( )
310104	BY	(310078)	310109	( )
310105	BY	(310090)	310110	( )

Class 311

311092	GW	311098	GW	311104	GW	311109	GW
311094	GW	311099	GW	311105	GW	311110	GW
311095	GW	311102	GW	311107	GW		
311097	GW	311103	GW	311108	GW		

Class 312/0

312701	CC	312711	CC	312721	CC
312702	CC	312712	CC	312722	CC
312703	CC	312713	CC	312723	CC
312704	CC	312714	CC	312724	CC
312705	CC	312715	CC	312725	CC
312706	CC	312716	CC	312726	CC
312707	CC	312717	CC	312727	CC
312708	CC	312718	CC	312728	CC
312709	CC	312719	CC	312729	CC
312710	CC	312720	CC	312730	CC

Class 312/1

312781	CC	312786	CC	312791	CC	312796	CC
312782	CC	312787	CC	312792	CC	312797	CC
312783	CC	312788	CC	312793	CC	312798	CC
312784	CC	312789	CC	312794	CC	312799	CC
312785	CC	312790	CC	312795	CC		

Class 313

313001	BY	313027	HE	313053	HE	
313002	BY	313028	HE	313054	HE	
313003	BY	313029	HE	313055	HE	
313004	BY	313030	HE	313056	HE	
313005	BY	313031	HE	313057	HE	
313006	BY	313032	HE	313058	HE	
313007	BY	313033	HE	313059	HE	
313008	BY	313034	HE	313060	HE	
313009	BY	313035	HE	313096	CC	(313061)
313010	BY	313036	HE	313097	CC	(313062)
313011	BY	313037	HE	313098	CC	(313063)
313012	BY	313038	HE	313099	CC	(313064)
313013	BY	313039	HE			
313014	BY	313040	HE			
313015	HE	313041	HE			
313016	HE	313042	HE			
313017	HE	313043	HE			
313018	HE	313044	HE			
313019	HE	313045	HE			
313020	HE	313046	HE			
313021	HE	313047	HE			
313022	HE	313048	HE			
313023	HE	313049	HE			
313024	HE	313050	HE			
313025	HE	313051	HE			
313026	HE	313052	HE			

Class 314

314201	GW	314205	GW	314209	GW	314213	GW
314202	GW	314206	GW	314210	GW	314214	GW
314203	GW	314207	GW	314211	GW	314215	GW
314204	GW	314208	GW	314212	GW	314216	GW

Class 315

315801	IL	315817	IL	315833	IL	315849	IL
315802	IL	315818	IL	315834	IL	315850	IL
315803	IL	315819	IL	315835	IL	315851	IL
315804	IL	315820	IL	315836	IL	315852	IL
315805	IL	315821	IL	315837	IL	315853	IL
315806	IL	315822	IL	315838	IL	315854	IL
315807	IL	315823	IL	315839	IL	315855	IL
315808	IL	315824	IL	315840	IL	315856	IL
315809	IL	315825	IL	315841	IL	315857	IL
315810	IL	315826	IL	315842	IL	315858	IL
315811	IL	315827	IL	315843	IL	315859	IL
315812	IL	315828	IL	315844	IL	315860	IL
315813	IL	315829	IL	315845	IL	315861	IL
315814	IL	315830	IL	315846	IL		
315815	IL	315831	IL	315847	IL		
315816	IL	315832	IL	315848	IL		

Class 317/1

317301	BY	317313	BY	317325	BY	317337	HE
317302	BY	317314	BY	317326	BY	317338	HE
317303	BY	317315	BY	317327	BY	317339	HE
317304	BY	317316	BY	317328	BY	317340	HE
317305	BY	317317	BY	317329	BY	317341	HE
317306	BY	317318	BY	317330	BY	317342	HE
317307	BY	317319	BY	317331	BY	317343	HE
317308	BY	317320	BY	317332	BY	317344	HE
317309	BY	317321	BY	317333	BY	317345	HE
317310	BY	317322	BY	317334	BY	317346	HE
317311	BY	317323	BY	317335	BY	317347	HE
317312	BY	317324	BY	317336	HE	317348	HE

Class 317/2

317349	HE	317356	HE	317363	HE	317370	HE
317350	HE	317357	HE	317364	HE	317371	HE
317351	HE	317358	HE	317365	HE	317372	HE
317352	HE	317359	HE	317366	HE		
317353	HE	317360	HE	317367	HE		
317354	HE	317361	HE	317368	HE		
317355	HE	317362	HE	317369	HE		

Class 318

318250	GW	318256	GW	318262	GW	318268	GW
318251	GW	318257	GW	318263	GW	318269	GW
318252	GW	318258	GW	318264	GW	318270	GW
318253	GW	318259	GW	318265	GW		
318254	GW	318260	GW	318266	GW		
318255	GW	318261	GW	318267	GW		

Class 319

319001	SU	319021	SU	319041	SU	319061	
319002	SU	319022	SU	319042	SU	319062	
319003	SU	319023	SU	319043	SU	319063	
319004	SU	319024	SU	319044	SU	319064	
319005	SU	319025	SU	319045	SU	319065	
319006	SU	319026	SU	319046	SU	319066	
319007	SU	319027	SU	319047	SU	319067	
319008	SU	319028	SU	319048	SU	319068	
319009	SU	319029	SU	319049	SU	319069	
319010	SU	319030	SU	319050	SU	319070	
319011	SU	319031	SU	319051	SU	319071	
319012	SU	319032	SU	319052	SU	319072	
319013	SU	319033	SU	319053	SU	319073	
319014	SU	319034	SU	319054	SU	319074	
319015	SU	319035	SU	319055	SU	319075	
319016	SU	319036	SU	319056	SU	319076	
319017	SU	319037	SU	319057	SU	319077	
319018	SU	319038	SU	319058	SU	319078	
319019	SU	319039	SU	319059	SU	319079	
319020	SU	319040	SU	319060	SU	319080	

Class 320 (3-Car units ordered for Strathclyde PTA Glasgow)

320	320	320
320	320	320

Class 321

321301	IL	321304	IL	321307	IL	321310	IL
321302	IL	321305	IL	321308	IL	321311	
321303	IL	321306	IL	321309	IL	321312	

321313	321328	321343	321358
321314	321329	321344	321359
321315	321330	321345	321360
321316	321331	321346	321361
321317	321332	321347	321362
321318	321333	321348	321363
321319	321334	321349	321364
321320	321335	321350	321365
321321	321336	321351	321366
321322	321337	321352	321367
321323	321338	321353	321368
321324	321339	321354	321369
321325	321340	321355	321370
321326	321341	321356	321371
321327	321342	321357	

Class 322 (4-Car Units ordered for Liverpool St.-Stansted Airport)

322	322
322	322
322	

Class 456 (2-Car Units on order)

456	456	456	456
456	456	456	456
456	456	456	456
456	456	456	456
456	456	456	456
456	456	456	456

Class 507

507001	HR	507010	HR	507019	HR	507028	HR
507002	HR	507011	HR	507020	HR	507029	HR
507003	HR	507012	HR	507021	HR	507030	HR
507004	HR	507013	HR	507022	HR	507031	HR
507005	HR	507014	HR	507023	HR	507032	HR
507006	HR	507015	HR	507024	HR	507033	HR
507007	HR	507016	HR	507025	HR		
507008	HR	507017	HR	507026	HR		
507009	HR	507018	HR	507027	HR		

Class 508

508101	BD	508112	BD	508123	BD	508134	BD
508102	BD	508113	BD	508124	BD	508135	BD
508103	BD	508114	BD	508125	BD	508136	BD
508104	BD	508115	BD	508126	BD	508137	BD
508105	BD	508116	BD	508127	BD	508138	BD
508106	BD	508117	BD	508128	BD	508139	HR
508107	BD	508118	BD	508129	BD	508140	HR
508108	BD	508119	BD	508130	BD	508141	HR
508109	BD	508120	BD	508131	BD	508142	HR
508110	BD	508121	BD	508132	BD	508143	HR
508111	BD	508122	BD	508133	BD		

DEPARTMENTAL UNITS

Current No.	Former No.	Description.	Allocation.
DB 975007	E79018		
DB 975008	E79612	Ultrasonic Test Train	RG
RDB 975010	M79900	Lab.Coach"IRIS"	RTC
TDB 975023	W55001	Route Learning Car	OO
TDB 975025	S60755	General Manager's Saloon	SL
ADB 975032	M75165	CM&EE Test Coach "MARS"	SH
TDB 975042	M55019	Route Learning Car	BY
RDB 975089	M50396		
RDB 975090	M56162	Trim Track Recording Unit Lab.5	RTC
TDB 975227	M55017	Route Learning Car	TS
DB 975349	E51116	Inspection Saloon	CA
ADB 975386	S60750	Tilting Test Lab.4	RTC
DB 975539	E56101	Inspection Saloon	CA
TDB 975540	W55016	Route Learning Car	OO
ADB 975586	S10907		
ADB 975587	S10908	Deicing Unit 004	EH
ADB 975588	S10981		
ADB 975589	S10982	Deicing Unit 005	WD
ADB 975590	S10833		
ADB 975591	S10834	Deicing Unit 006	WD
ADB 975592	S10993		
ADB 975593	S12659	Deicing Unit 007	GI
ADB 975594	S12658		

ADB 975595	S10994	Deicing Unit 003	SU
ADB 975596	S10844		
ADB 975597	S10897	Deicing Unit 008	AF
ADB 975598	S10989		
ADB 975599	S10990	Deicing Unit 009	BI
ADB 975600	S10988		
ADB 975601	S10843	Deicing Unit 010	BI
ADB 975602	S10991		
ADB 975603	S10992	Deicing Unit 011	RE
ADB 975604	S10939		
ADB 975605	S10940	Deicing Unit 012	FR
DB 975637	E56300	E.R.General Manager's Saloon	CA
TDB 975659	W55035	Route Learning Car	OO
DB 975664	E51122	E.R.General Manager's Saloon	CA
ADB 975844	S64305		
ADB 975849	S62426		
ADB 975850	S62429		
ADB 975851	S64304	Experimental Unit 057	SUu
ADB 975896	S11387		
ADB 975897	S11388	Deicing Unit 013	RE
ADB 977048	E56142	Sandite Coach	BX
ADB 977052	M56145	Sandite Coach	BY
ADB 977068	S14549		
ADB 977069	S16029	Stores Unit 019	SG
TDB 977123	E51286	Route Learning Car	CA
TDB 977124	E51296	Route Learning Car	CA
TDB 977125	E56444	Route Learning Car	CA
TDB 977126	E56445	Route Learning Car	CA
ADB 977290	S65318		
ADB 977291	S65324	Stores Unit 018	SG
ADB 977296	S65319		
ADB 977297	S77108	SR Tractor Unit 050	SH
ADB 977304	S65317		
ADB 977305	S65322	SR Tractor Unit 021	WD
DB 977335	S76277	Support Coach for DB 999550	SR
DB 977336	S76278	Support Coach for DB 999550	SR
ADB 977345	M61178		
ADB 977346	M75178	Sandite Unit	BD
ADB 977347	M61180		
ADB 977348	M75180	Sandite Unit	BD
ADB 977349	M61183		
ADB 977350	M75183	Sandite Unit	BD
ADB 977362	S10392	Trailer Deicing Coach	FR

ADB 977363	S10399	Trailer Deicing Coach	BI
ADB 977364	S10400	Trailer Deicing Coach	BM
ADB 977365	S10726	Deicing Unit 001(part)	SU
ADB 977366	S10500	Deicing Unit 002	
ADB 977367	S10497	Deicing Unit 002	SU
ADB 977368	S10499	Deicing Unit 001(part)	SU
ADB 977376	S60002		
ADB 977377	S60003		
ADB 977379	S60504	Sandite Unit 066	SU
ADB 977385	M61148		
ADB 977386	M75189	Sandite Unit	WN
DB 977391	E51433	Power Cars for Ultrasonic	RTC
DB 977392	E53167	Test Train	RTC
DB 977393	E53246	as above (waiting conversion)	Cathays
DB 977394	S65316	Traction Unit for DB 999550(waiting conversion)	
TDB 977466	W54286	Sandite Coach	CF
TDB 977486	W54285	Sandite Coach	CF
ADB 977505	S65321	Test Unit 054	SH
ADB 977506	S65323	Test Unit 053	SH
ADB 977507	S77110	Test Unit 054	SH
ADB 977508	S77112	Test Unit 053	SH
RDB 977527	Sc48204	Tilting Test Vehicle (APT Lab.2)	RTC
ADB 977531	S14047	Deicing Unit 015	WD
ADB 977532	S14048		
ADB 977533	S14273	Deicing Unit 016	WD
ADB 977534	S14384		
ADB 977535	E53259		
ADB 977536	E53295	Sandite Unit	HT
TDB 977554	M54182	Sandite Unit	BX
TDB 977555	M54183	Sandite Unit	BS
ADB 977559	S65313	Stores Unit 026	SG
ADB 977560	S65320		
ADB 977566	S65312	Stores Unit 017	SG
ADB 977567	S65314		
ADB 977578	S77101>		
ADB 977579	S77109>	Sandite Unit(waiting conversion)	SU
ADB 977598	E75080>		
ADB 977599	E61073>		
ADB 977600	E75061>	Sandite Unit 996	CC
ADB 977601	E75211>		
ADB 977602	E61228>		
ADB 977603	E75035>	Sandite Unit 997	IL

ADB 977604	E75077>		
ADB 977605	E61062>		
ADB 977606	E75070>	Sandite Unit 998	EM
TDB 977607	Sc51464	Route Learner/Sandite Unit	ED
TDB 977608	Sc51525	Route Learner/Sandite Unit	ED
ADB 977609	S65414	Tractor Unit(waiting conversion)	SR
ADB 977610	S77136	Tractor Unit(waiting conversion)	SR
ADB 977611	E51824	Sandite Unit	NL
ADB 977612	E51838	Sandite Unit	NL
ADB 977613	E51826	Sandite Unit	NL
ADB 977614	E52076	Sandite Unit	NL
ADB 977615	W54281	Sandite Unit(waiting conversion)	LA
DB999600			
DB999601		CE Track Recording Train	RTC
DB 999602	S62483	Instrument Coach	RTC
DB 999603	S62482	Instrument Coach (waiting conversion) Cathays	
RDB 999507		Wickham Built Laboratory	RTC

OXFORD PUBLISHING COMPANY

Complete List of Current Titles

Title	No	Price
★ 30A – Steam on Stratford Shed	T454	9.95
Banbury and Cheltenham Railway	T845	9.95
Barry Locomotive Phenomenon, The	T410	14.95
Big Four Cameraman	T363	18.95
▶ Big Four Remembered	T463	19.95
Bishop's Stortford, Dunmow & Braintree (PB)	T142	4.95
BR Wagons Vol. 1	T203	18.95
Bridges for Modellers	T226	12.95
Brill Tramway	T218	11.95
▶ British Marshalling Yards	T367	19.95
British Rail in Camera	T368	12.95
British Rail Main Line Diesel Locomotives	T318	19.95
British Rail Operations in the 1980s	T248	9.95
British Rail Spotter's Companion 11th Ed.	T436	1.50
▶ British Rail Spotter's Companion 12th Ed.	T456	1.95

BR Maps & Gazetteer Revised Ed. (1825-1985)	T294	12.95
BR Standard Steam Locomotives	T158	12.95
Buchan Line (PB)	T179	4.95
Cambrian Companionship	T344	12.95
▶ Capital Steam	T412	14.95
Chester to Holyhead Railway	T216	14.95
Class 52s: A Tribute to the Westerns	T424	14.95
Class 58 Life & Times Series	T422	12.95
Cleobury Mortimer & Ditton Priors Railway	T053	9.95
Cowbridge Railway	T284	9.95
Crewe Works	T395	12.95
Didcot, Newbury & Southampton Railway	T149	12.95
Diesel Shunter	T108	12.95
Diesel Traction, 35 Years of Main Line	T171	9.95
Diesel and Electrics on Shed Vol. 5 Southern	T044	9.95
Diesels and Semaphores	T345	9.95
Diesels in South Wales	T295	9.95
Diesels in the East Midlands	T302	9.95
Diesels in the North East	T262	8.95
Diesels in the North West	T350	9.95
Diesels in the West Midlands	T357	10.95
Diesels in the White Rose County	T417	11.95
Diesels Nationwide Vol. 2	T068	8.95
Diesels Nationwide Vol. 3	T113	8.95
Diesels Nationwide Vol. 4	T114	8.95
Diesels on the Regions – Eastern	T230	9.95
Diesels on the Regions – London Midland	T250	9.95
Diesels on the Regions – Scottish	T253	9.95
Diesels on the Regions – Southern	T243	10.95
Diesels on the Regions – Western	T221	9.95
Diesels Over the Settle & Carlisle	T119	9.95
East Anglian Steam, 55 Years of	T182	9.95
Electric Traction, 100 years of	T325	14.95
Engines Good and Bad (PB)	T326	4.95
Footplateman Remembers the Southern (PB)	T340	4.95
Forest of Dean Railways	T167	11.95
Gleneagles to Glastonbury	T351	9.95
Glyn Valley Tramway	T286	9.95
Great Central, Echoes of the	T411	14.95
Great Western A. E. C. Diesel Railcars	T139	19.95
Great Western Absorbed Engines	T874	17.95
Great Western at Swindon Works	T177	14.95
Great Western Coaches Appendix Vol. 1	T084	18.95

Great Western Coaches Appendix Vol. 2	T154	17.95
Great Western Engine Sheds 1837-1947	T019	14.95
Great Western Engines Vol. 1	T398	17.95
Great Western Engines Vol. 2	T399	17.95
Great Western Reflections (PB)	T332	4.95
Great Western Remembered	T204	9.95
Great Western Signalling	T346	12.95
Great Western Stations Vol. 2	T015	15.95
Great Western Stations Vol. 4	T191	19.95
Great Western Steam Album	T386	12.95
Great Western, Around the Branch Lines No. 2	T213	9.95
▷ GWR Freight Wagons & Loads	T155	14.95
GWR Sheds in Camera	T385	12.95
Highland Miscellany	T309	10.95
Hobson's Choice	T370	8.95
Isle of Wight Railways Remembered	T212	9.95
John Ashman FRPS Rail Portfolio	T416	12.95
Kenning Collection	T813	3.95
Lancs & Yorks Railway Miscellany	T188	10.95
Lines to Torrington	T145	14.95
LMS Architecture	T083	18.95
LMS in the West Midlands	T259	9.95
LMS Locomotives Vol. 1 General Review	T087	19.95
LMS Locomotives Vol. 2 Western & Central	T264	19.95
LMS Locomotives Vol. 3 Northern	T266	19.95
LMS Miscellany Vol. 2	T290	10.95
LMS Miscellany Vol. 3	T383	12.95
LMS Road Vehicles	T174	12.95
LMS Sheds in Camera	T274	9.95
LMS Stations Vol. 2	T330	17.95
LMS Wagons Vol. 2	T255	12.95
LNER Constituent Signalling	T146	12.95
LNER Sheds in Camera	T324	10.95
LNER Wagons	T892	12.95
LNWR Engines	T209	19.95
LNWR Miscellany Vol. 2	T070	9.95
LNWR Recalled	T392	16.95
LNWR Signalling	T147	12.95
Locos, Men and Steam Memories	T316	7.95
Manchester Ship Canal Railways	T288	15.95
Merthyr, Tredegar & Abergavenny Railway	T339	14.95
Midland Carriages	T291	14.95
Midland in Gloucestershire	T301	14.95

Midland Railway Architecture	T320	10.95
Midland Wagons Vol. 1	T040	11.95
N.E.R. Locomotives	T323	19.95
Nameplates of the Big Four	T843	10.95
North Eastern Branch Line Termini	T219	14.95
North Eastern Branch Lines	T189	9.95
North Wales Steam Vol. 1	T074	10.95
North Wales Steam Vol. 2	T305	12.95
Northern Steam Remembered	T387	10.95
Nostalgic Days (PB)	T079	2.95
Once Upon a Line Vol. 1 (Isle of Wight)	T277	10.95
Once Upon a Line Vol. 2 (Isle of Wight)	T280	10.95
Oxford to Cambridge Railway Vol. 1	T120	9.95
Oxford to Cambridge Railway Vol. 2	T121	9.95
Portishead Branch (PB)	T190	4.95
Power of the 33s	T157	9.95
Power of the 40s	T033	9.95
Power of the A1s, A2s and A3s	T133	9.95
Power of the A4s	T032	11.95
Power of the AC Electrics	T246	12.95
Power of the B17s & B2s	T396	11.95
Power of the Black Fives	T238	14.95
Power of the BR Standard Pacifics	T067	9.95
Power of the Bulleid Pacifics	T082	9.95
Power of the 31s	T064	9.95
Power of the 56s	T150	9.95
Power of the Deltics	T897	9.95
Power of the HSTs	T186	9.95
Power of the Royal Scots	T175	9.95
Pregrouping Trains on BR-LMS Companies	T394	11.95
Pregrouping Trains on BR-LNER Companies	T315	9.95
Pregrouping in the West Midlands	T328	9.95
Private Owner Wagons (Glos. C & W Co.)	T124	12.95
Profile of the 40s	T144	6.95
Profile of the 47s	T240	8.95
Profile of the A4s	T354	7.95
Profile of the Class 20s	T244	6.95
Profile of the 24s and 25s	T135	8.95
Profile of the 50s	T233	6.95
Profile of the 76s and 77s	T156	6.95
Profile of the Duchesses	T176	8.95
Profile of the Peaks	T165	6.95
Profile of the Southern Moguls	T314	8.95

Profile of the Warships	T279	6.95
Profile of the Westerns	T116	8.95
Rail Atlas of Great Britain & Ireland 5th Ed	T419	9.95
▶ Railfreight today	T439	12.95
★ Railway Research, 25 years of	T441	12.95
▷ Scottish Branch Lines	T005	9.95
Railway Elegance (Western Region Diesels in Colour)	T349	12.95
Settle & Carlisle Rly Stations & Structures	T360	15.95
Signal Box (A Pictorial History)	T224	19.95
Signalling Days (PB)	T118	3.95
Somerset & Dorset from the Footplate	T403	11.95
Somerset & Dorset in the 60s Vol. 3	T160	9.95
Somerset & Dorset Railway Track Layouts	T003	14.95
Somerset & Dorset (English Cross Country Railway)	T833	12.95
Somewhere Along the Line	T880	14.95
South Wales, Steam in Vol. 2	T152	9.95
South Wales, Steam in Vol. 3	T169	9.95
South Wales, Steam in Vol. 4	T285	9.95
Southern in Hampshire & Dorset	T289	9.95
Southern in Kent & Sussex	T273	9.95
Southern in Surrey & Berkshire	T426	10.95
Southern Mainline Cameraman	T365	12.95
Southern Metals, On	T215	9.95
Southern Wagons Vol. 1	T207	12.95
Southern Wagons Vol. 2	T220	12.95
Southern West of Salisbury	T341	9.95
Southern, Around the Branch Lines No. 1	T159	9.95
Southern Cross Country Routes	T267	9.95
Sunset of British Steam	T163	9.95
Swindon Works Apprentice in Steam	T380	10.95
Taff Vale Miscellany	T414	12.95
Teign Valley Line (PB)	T194	5.95
Thaxted Branch (PB)	T184	4.95
Thro' the Lens (GWR Official Photographs)	T312	8.95
Thro' the Lens (PB)	T356	4.95
Tollesbury Branch	T327	10.95
Trans-Pennine Rail Routes	T307	14.95
Treacy's LMS	T381	15.95
Tribute to the Western	T362	9.95
Twilight of Scottish Steam	T391	10.95
Twixt London and Bristol	T364	9.95
Visions of Steam (Industrial Steam)	T031	9.95
West Country China Clay Trains	T299	12.95

Weymouth Harbour Tramway	**T304**	12.95
Yesterday's Railwayman (PB)	**T331**	4.95

(PB) Paperback
★ Forthcoming publication
▶ New title
▷ Re-issued title